UNVEILING THE POWER

— OF THE —

HEART

A CHANNELED TEXT

DARREN MARC

ISBN: Paperback 979-8-2183-9877-4
ISBN: EBook 979-8-8937-9312-3

TABLE OF CONTENTS

A NOTE FROM THE AUTHOR

Hi friends,

These channeled transmissions came through me over the course of several months in my morning meditations. The art of channeling is an uplifting experience through which one raises their personal vibration to meet the vibration of the "guides" who want to come forth. We are all channels whether we recognize it or not. We are all channels for the love, light, and wisdom of God (or whatever you prefer to label that which cannot be labeled). We are all here to share our gifts with the world and to make it a better place. Every time I channeled the words and energy of The Teachers of The Light, I felt uplifted, supported, and nourished. I hope reading these words, and feeling the energy of these loving guides, does the same for you. Please visit my website at www.awakenwithdarren.com to see what private and group offerings I have available, as I'd love to meet you in the space of the heart.

Love & Light,
Darren

THE GREAT SHIFT

Chapter 1

Good morning, friends. It is with great love that we greet you. Many of you have been experiencing shifts that are leading you to a greater understanding and a greater knowingness of who it is you are. And it needn't be said, but we will say it: This who you are. It is much more vast than the name that you call yourself. For that can be quite limiting, can it not? So we would say that this shift that we are speaking of is a shift that is taking you outside of the boxes that you have lived in. And you are beginning to know more of yourself, more of your true self, that is beyond how you have previously experienced yourself.

The shifts that you are experiencing in your own lives are being experienced by every human being on this planet.

In the past, we have labeled this time the time of awakening, the great awakening. But it might also be labeled the great shift, the great shift of consciousness, the great shift into a knowingness of who it is you are by way of direct experience. Not by way of what you have been told by anybody outside of yourself, but by way of direct experience.

This is the way, friends; it is the only way. You cannot get to know yourself by being told by anybody else who it is you are, what it is you can do, and what it is you cannot do. True understanding of who you are, in your entirety, must come by way of direct experience. And every little shift that occurs within yourself is leading you back home to know yourself in all of your entirety.

And so it is, friends, if it has not come yet, it will come very soon: a day in which you no longer seek anything that is outside of yourself. Meaning, you will no longer have to seek out the opinions of others as to who it is you are, or what it is you should be doing in your life, because you will know. You will know in your heart and you will know in your spirit. And you will know because you will feel it.

You will have a direct experience of who it is you are.

You will have a direct experience of your spirit leading you where you are meant to be in your life. And you will have a direct experience of knowing that wherever you are in the present moment, that is okay too. You will have a direct experience that it is good to celebrate that as well. Meaning, that it is good to celebrate the journey that you are on, rather than being focused on the destination itself.

There is so much happening on your planet right now, friends, that it is beyond the understanding of your intellect, yes? Your intellect cannot figure it out. So we encourage you not to even attempt to. Just create space for all that is happening to happen. And see things as they are, friends. If there is darkness that is being revealed from within you or if there is darkness that you see around you, know that it is only possible to see this darkness by way of the light that is flooding onto the planet right now, from the source of creation.

Dear ones, you are about to discover, if you have not yet, that you are this source that we speak of! And that the separation between you and this source, or this "god" that you call it, was a belief that was instilled upon your consciousness many eons ago. And so, the greatest shift of all that is occurring by way of all these little shifts, is a dismantling of this belief system, a crumbling of this belief system, a *shattering* of this belief system, yes? And a direct experience of yourself as that which you are, not separate from, but *one* with source.

Then you will know the potential that every other human being on the planet has to also experience oneness with source energy. And you will reach out your hand, yes? And you will uplift others who are ready to be uplifted so that they too might know this truth.

> *And so that creator's vision, which is the vision*
> *that comes from within you, will be fulfilled.*

We have spoken of this vision many times, friends, yes? It is the dimension that you call heaven becoming manifested on this planet Earth. And know that it is not a place residing outside of you that you must get to when you leave your body, and that you will only be admitted to if you have lived a particular kind of life. No, it is not like this at all, friends. You will come to know that heaven is a dimension, or a plane, or a reality, or a frequency, or whatever it is you wish to call it, that becomes available for you to experience right here and right now in your physical form, by way of the shifts that are occurring in your life, by the raising of your vibration, and by the raising of vibrations for all on this planet. And then it will be done as it is already done in our eyes. From our perspective it cannot not be done, for it is happening right now.

The channel has been listening to another channel! And the energy that comes through that particular channel often speaks of humanity having crossed a threshold. And you have indeed, friends: know this to be true in your heart and in your spirit. For it is true, meaning all will be well now.

Trust in the process that is happening for yourself and all of humanity.

You are all being led home to experience the truth that is within yourselves, which will lead to the creation, to the manifestation, to the unveiling…mmm what a powerful word that is… of the frequency and vibration of heaven manifested on Earth.

We will leave you with this, friends. The veil is being broken. This is why we said the word "unveiling" was so powerful. And we say that it is happening. The veil is being dismantled. That which you have not seen in the past is becoming seen again. All dimensions are becoming available for you to experience here and now. The separation is coming to an end. And as we see it, it is over already. For this is the river you are on. All will be one in the name of love. Many blessings, my friends.

RETREATING INTO YOUR HEART

Chapter 2

Blessings, dear ones. There is a sun shining in your heart. For some, it's just a sparkle. But for others, it is so vast it covers the entire universe and then some. This is the light we wish to help you to cultivate. Many of you feel overburdened by the circumstances in your lives. So, this particular chapter will be devoted to making room for spirit in your life. It's only by making room for spirit that your heart will shine like the sun.

The channel is thinking of a closet, and it's a perfect analogy. Many of you have closets that are full – so full of your thoughts and your obligations that the mere thought of adding a spiritual practice into your life is overwhelming. Just the thought of it makes you say "no." Many of you have to-do lists that seem to last for an eternity. But we want to make this message very clear to you. And perhaps it's even the most important thing we'll say in this entire book:

There is nothing more important than connecting to your heart.

One of the best ways to do this is to still your mind through spiritual practice. Many of you will say, "Oh, but that isn't what's most important. My friends are most important. My family is most important. My job is most important. My health is most important." We will be bold and say that all these things will improve if you dedicate some time to spiritual practice. And at the very least, you must make your spiritual practice as important as everything else.

We begin here before talking about anything else because it is the foundation you must build your life upon. Without this spiritual practice, you are like a leaf blowing in the wind. You have no control over your mind, and it's very difficult to experience your heart's greatness.

The channel has something on his mind, and we feel it's fitting to mention it here. The love we speak about, the love that is in the depths of your heart, is vaster than the love you feel for a partner or the love you feel for a friend. That love is limiting. As beautiful, as glorious, as expansive, as delightful as it is, the love we speak of is even bigger and better because it's a love that has no preferences. It is a love that is not reserved for any one particular person. It is a love for all. We will come back to this word "all" many times, for it is quite an important word.

If you feel a resonance with what we've said so far, and you wish to continue along this journey with us, then make a commitment to yourself and to us. We, the Teachers of the Light, are all *love*. So, we won't be angry if you break your commitment. We have nothing but love for you, as does the creator him-herself. There are no rules here. This is not a place of worship where someone tells you to do something in a particular way, or you won't get it right. We have only great love for you. So out of this love, we make suggestions that we feel will be quite beneficial for you. And so the suggestion, this commitment that we would be very flattered if you would embark upon, is to retreat into your heart for at least fifteen minutes, twice per day.

The channel remembers something an acting teacher once said:

The best way to love yourself is to make a commitment and to stick with it.

We agree wholeheartedly with this statement. The commitment, my friends, is to take fifteen minutes, twice a day, to still your mind and connect to your heart. Much like a turtle sticks his head inside his shell, you must do the same. You must withdraw your senses from the outside world to see what is inside of you. It's the only way to see everything that is there. You can get a glimpse of it through your experiences in the outside world. But we want you to get more than a glimpse. We want you to see the totality of who you are. And then you must weave this experience of who you are into the outside world. You must go in and out, in and out, in and out, much like the waves of the ocean. If you sit and watch it, you will see. It goes in, it goes out. It has this constant movement. It goes out toward the sand, toward the world, but then it retreats into itself.

We want you to do this as well. We want you to retreat into yourself as often as possible. For it is here, inside of you, that you will find the holy grail of life, the greatest prize. It is a prize that is even better than winning an academy award. It is a prize that is much better than being well-known for your work. It is even a prize that is a greater reward than having a successful, loving relationship with your partner and your children. We encourage you to do all these things if it is in your heart to do so. But seek what is inside of yourself.

After many years of practice, the channel has become quite adept at this. He calls it "meditation," but we prefer to call it "retreat." When you go on retreat, you go to get away from the outside world, to be by yourself, to be quiet, to be still, and to listen. And it is here, in this stillness, that you have your revelations, that wisdom arises mysteriously from inside of you. Sometimes, you do not even know where it came from, but there it is. It is here, in stillness, that you also begin to strip away the conditioning and the programming that has been placed, like a filter, over your heart. For now, make this commitment of going on a retreat twice a day for fifteen minutes per sitting.

Fifteen minutes or more is when you actually give yourself enough time to experience what is within you. You do not need to set an alarm clock; this is a distraction. Trust yourself to know when the time is up, and then open your eyes and stick your head back out of your shell and return to all there is to do in the outside world. We promise you'll lose no time. Instead, you'll gain time. For every fifteen minutes you spend within yourself, you will find that you mysteriously have more time to do what you need to do.

We, through the channel, are laughing because you're probably saying to yourselves, "No way. I don't believe it. Time is time." But you'll see. It won't happen overnight. This practice of retreat will bring improvement to every area of your life. You will no longer feel as rushed. You will actually get more done because you'll feel more relaxed. You'll be amazed at how productive you can be and how much more focused your mind is when you're relaxed.

One of the benefits of sacred retreat is that you'll cultivate a state of relaxation that will begin to permeate every moment of your day. Perhaps this relaxation will become such a part of you that you'll begin to see life as we see it: Sacred. And when we say that we see life as sacred, we don't mean isolated moments of it. We do not mean only the good moments. We mean every moment. We mean every breath is a sacred one. In your current state of mind, it's impossible to experience this sacredness. This is why it is incredibly important to go on retreat.

The more you go on sacred retreat, the more the world will begin to look different through your eyes.

It will be the same world, but you'll experience it much differently. This is why every spiritual teacher has taught, in one way or another, this practice we call going on "retreat" and that the channel calls "meditation." Sacred retreat is the first thing children should be taught when they go to school. And so, if by chance, one of you who is reading this is a teacher (and we know who you are because we see you reading this book already), perhaps you'll be so brave to bring this practice into every school.

This is the essential practice that every child needs to learn from the very beginning. When this happens, there will be much more peace in the world and less violence. They will connect with each other in a new way. Right now, your children feel incredibly isolated and separate from each other. This is the affliction of today: separation.

We cry for these children because they feel so separate. This will resonate with many of you because of the experiences your own children are having, some of whom openly share it with you. Others keep it within themselves because they're too embarrassed to speak their truth. We have digressed, but it was an important point to make. And often you will find us digressing a little bit. But trust there is a divine flow to these words and that everything is in perfect order, just as it is in the universe.

*Even if things look chaotic, there is a divine
order to all that is occurring.*

You might look outside your window and say to yourself, "Oh my god, the world has gone to hell!" We smile as we say that because we want you to understand there's a lightness and a joy in our words that the channel feels himself as he speaks them. But know indeed, friends, that everything is just as it should be in this moment. It can be no other way. And all are heading toward the light. Some must get pretty deep into the darkness to get there. But all are going to the same place.

When you look outside, and everything looks chaotic, and it seems like the world is turning upside down, and everybody is going crazy, including Mother Earth sometimes, trust that everything is alright. That is not to say that you shouldn't stand up for what you believe in, but at the same time, have a deep sense of trust that all is well in the universe.

*Now we would like to give you instructions
for going on sacred retreat.*

We encourage you to stick to your practice. In the same way it is likely that you do not miss a day brushing your teeth, use the same diligence in this practice of retreat. This is a lifelong practice, my friends. If you could imagine a flower that blossoms for an entire lifespan, this practice of retreat is much like that. Every time you go on retreat, you open a little bit more.

The practice of retreat is quite simple. We invite you to create a sacred space solely devoted to retreat. And when we say the word "solely," we mean it. It isn't very often we get too firm because we like to keep it very light. But we are quite adamant about this - about all of you creating a sacred space solely for retreat.

Many of you might say, "There is nowhere I can do it. There is no space in my house." We say, make the space. You will know what to do intuitively. If you would like to put a candle there, then do it. If you would like to put a photograph or photographs of inspiring spiritual teachers that have come before us, absolutely do this. If you would like to put an item there that helps you connect to the divine that is both within you and all around you, then do that. And if it is simply a chair or a stool or a cushion all by itself, that is perfectly fine as well.

Once you have created your sacred space, and before you enter into it, make sure there's nothing, and we mean *absolutely nothing*, that will distract you from your retreat. Power off your phone. Power off your computer. Do whatever it is you need to do to ensure you won't feel distracted. Every time you go inside of yourself, it is a sacred event.

Enter into your sacred space with reverence, for it is indeed a sacred space designed by you to cocoon yourself into, with the light of your own heart. As you enter your sacred space, take a moment to honor it in your heart.

Be grateful that it exists because this is your sanctuary.

And it is yours and yours only. Indeed, if there is somebody else who says, "I'd like to check out your sacred retreat space," say, "No, it is my space." Smile brightly at them and encourage them to create their own space.

When you're in your sacred space, make yourself comfortable. Put yourself in a comfortable seat. Do not slouch as if you are about to watch your favorite TV show or eat nachos. But do find a comfortable seat with your spine fairly erect. It doesn't have to be straight like the Empire State Building, but it should be fairly erect.

Close your eyes. Rest your hands in the balance mudra - fingers and palms resting on top of each other with the tops of the thumbs touching. This is the mudra that bridges heaven and earth. For in your sacred space, you are indeed uniting the higher realms with the Earth plane and bringing them together into your heart. As an alternative to the balance mudra, you can simply rest your hands on your knees or thighs.

Pay attention to your breath. Let it be incredibly soft, like a baby's breath. And simply watch it. That's all. We told you it would be very simple. As the channel very often tells his yoga students, do not attempt to change the pattern of your breath. Simply observe it. If and when a thought pops up in your mind, that's alright. Notice it. Just as you notice your breath, notice the thought. And then draw your awareness back to your breath.

Do this for fifteen minutes. When you intuitively sense it's time to come out of retreat, bring your hands together in front of your heart center. Thank yourself for showing up to your retreat. And then out loud, state three things that you are grateful for in your life, beginning with the words "I AM grateful for…."

These two words, "I AM," are incredibly important words.

There will be more meditations to come. Trust, my friends, that these meditations will take you somewhere. But it is not as you think. They will not take you from place A to place B. They will not help you to manifest a Rolls Royce or a private jet or a mansion. There are certainly other techniques you can use to do that—but don't focus on manifesting things yet.

Rather than taking you from place A to place B, these practices are meant to bring you back into your heart. And it is there you will find all, and again we do mean *all*, that you have ever sought. Everything you want is there waiting for you, residing in the four holy chambers of your heart. All the love you seek, all the light you seek, and all the joy you seek are all there waiting for you. And thus, this practice of retreat is another step forward into your heart.

Be patient with yourselves, dear ones.

A big problem in this world you are living in is that many people want instant gratification. The world is now wired like that, right? The channel knows he can go onto Amazon.com and the following day, he can have whatever he wants, even if it's just a roll of toilet paper. If there is information you seek, you can jump online and get it instantly.

However, the greatest prizes in life require some effort and some time to accomplish. And indeed, it is an accomplishment to experience what we want you to experience. We promise you this. You will all, and we mean *all*, get there. Many of you will get there in this incarnation because of the quickening that is happening on this planet.

So be patient with yourself, be kind to yourself, be committed, be devoted, and you will reap the harvest you seek. There will come a day and time where it all falls into place, and you'll have found what it is you're looking for. The channel will be holding monthly live meditations, and we invite you to join him because our energies will be present for these meditations—for these retreats.

We will close by saying blessings, dear ones.

You are so incredibly loved.

If you do not feel that love right now, you will soon. Love is coming for all. Know that we are with you always, and we shine our light toward you and all of humanity at this time of great awakening for all. And we encourage you to embark upon the practices we share in this book for forty days.

Make that commitment to yourselves and do it out of love. Do it because you have great love for yourself—not because we're telling you to, not because you think it's the right thing to do, and not because you want to experiment with it just to see. Do it because you have great love for yourself, and out of that great love, you want to do something to uplift yourself, to raise your level of consciousness, and to help yourself discover the god-presence within you.

The channel remembers a story he heard about a meditation teacher who used to walk around with a whip. He would whip a student if he or she made the slightest movement during the meditation. We are not those kinds of teachers. We do not carry a whip. We only carry love in our hearts and a smile on our light body faces. We are filled with joy to be of service. We are completely unattached as to whether you follow our guidance or not.

But we encourage you, wholeheartedly, out of the love we have for you, to make this commitment to yourselves. It is only by engaging in these practices for a good amount of time that you will start to reap the benefits and that you will experience the shift we'd like you to experience. For that reason, we encourage you to commit to a forty-day practice.

It's likely that after the forty days, you'll feel inspired to continue without our coaxing. If you miss a day or two, it's perfectly fine. Simply continue. In fact, because we are teachers of great love, and we have a good sense of humor, we give you three permitted absences. We hope you'll be disciplined enough to go on sacred retreat thirty-seven out of forty days!

As this journey unfolds, the channel will include some additional practices that you can add to the practice we have introduced to you in this chapter. These additional practices are not meant to take the place of this essential practice, but rather to compliment it. The channel has many years of experience in various practices that help him to still his mind, access his heart, and connect to god. And so it is, every practice that he shares with you will be of great benefit to you. Blessings, dear ones.

2024: THE YEAR OF CHANGE

Chapter 3

What a delight it is to join you in the space of the heart. This space that we speak of so often, the space of the heart, has actually been a little elusive for the channel lately. The reason we are offering you, and him, this transmission is to help all of you locate this space in your heart. For even though you have heard it before, and you will hear it again, it is indeed the most pleasurable place to reside in human form.

It does not matter so much where you are and what you are doing. What is of importance, is that you are in that sacred space of the heart where love, compassion, and happiness reside.

For this is what all of you want, is it not? Your human selves say you want this or that. Perhaps you say you want this relationship, or this job, or this vacation, or this amount of money.

But what you really seek is to be in this space of love, compassion, and joy. This is what you all share as a collective.

Many of you have past hurts, the channel included. And so unconsciously, you have turned off your hearts because it is simply easier to not feel. And yet, there is a space in your heart, an energetic space of the heart, that actually exists beyond what we would call "human emotions." For many of you think that love is an emotion, but it is not. Love is a frequency, an energy, a vibration– not an emotion. We wish to guide you into the frequency of love. Thus, today's teaching is a very high-level, advanced teaching. One that should stand out to you and be re-read many times, perhaps every day, as part of your sacred retreat practice.

And so it is, dear ones, when you begin to settle into your sacred retreat practice, as the channel will share in his own words later, you may very well simply be noticing your breath. You will likely choose a location in the physical body where it's easier for you to be aware of the breath, most likely as it is moving in and out of the nostrils. And you begin there: this is step one.

But then, as your practice unfolds, you must have a subtle intention of dropping into your heart space, of allowing your intention to rest with your breath in your heart. And you may repeat these words now as you read them, and in your sacred retreat practice with your soft, relaxed, focused attention on your heart space:

I open my heart as much as I can in this present moment.
I open my heart as much as I can in this present moment.
I open my heart as much as I can in this present moment.

For some of you, this might actually be uncomfortable. Because as you place your awareness on your energetic heart, if there are heavier emotions (such as hurt, pain, sadness, or grief) in the body that has yet to be expressed, they may surface now to be expressed. This is simply part of the journey, of purifying the heart so you may be in love. So let those denser energies surface and release. You may then call upon us, The Teachers of The Light. When you do so, all of your personal guides and angels will be drawn toward you and will also help you to open your hearts.

Do this every day in your practice, dear ones, for this is what is missing from many modern-day teachings of meditation. Yes, the teachings are to still the mind and to be self-realized, to have direct communion, possibly even a union with god. But the teachers are not placing enough awareness on the heart center. And we tell you, dear ones, that this is the path to freedom. And all of you want to be free, do you not? Free from the shackles that bind you? Freedom is found in your hearts, to be in a pure, loving space.

And then, those who are meant to be drawn towards you, will more easily be drawn towards you. Those who are meant to stay away, will be more prone to stay away. And if someone comes into your life who is not an energetic match for you, for your wants, for your needs, and for the love that you are worthy of, you will simply be able to let that person go because you will have clear, strong, healthy boundaries.

And you will simply wait for somebody else to appear in your life who is a better match for you. This could be a friend, a partner, or a business relationship.

We also encourage you, dear ones, to seek out experiences in the outer world that also help you to open your hearts. This could be spending time with an animal that you are fond of. It could be spending time in nature and simply admiring the beauty of creation. It could be as simple as gazing towards the beauty of a flower. Simple things, dear ones. It needn't be too complex. It is child's play, is it not? For we want you to return to the innocence of your hearts.

The children have innocent hearts because they have yet to experience adulthood. They have yet to experience the ups and downs of life, the challenges that so often lead to someone closing off their heart. And so, if you can spend time around free-spirited, pure-hearted children– be it children of your own, or a friend's children, or children that you can mentor in some way– that would be beneficial as well.

There is so much love for you, dear ones, here in the higher realms, which are not much higher than you are. For there is an awakening of consciousness that is occurring on the planet, a shift. This shift is helping the entire planet, and all of humanity, rise in vibration, rise in frequency–up, up, up, towards the light, towards the god-head. Please re-read what we have just said–it is of incredible importance.

Mother Earth and all of humanity, is rising, rising, rising into the light, closer to the god-head, where there is tremendous unfathomable love that is had for each and every one of you and all of creation.

In your sacred retreats, dear ones, as you still your minds and access your hearts, be with the intention to rise, rise, rise into the light. As you rise, rise, rise into the light dear ones, you will feel lighter. You will feel more connected with god. You will feel like you are home in the light even though you are still walking in a physical body on planet Earth.

And naturally, you will start to carry others with you. Your new high vibration will help others to find that similar vibration. Which is why we also ask you to start teaching sacred retreat in your own home once you have finished reading this book. Even if it is to be shared with just one or two or three people once per week, or once every two weeks, please do this. For it is time, dear ones. It is time for the frequency of all of humanity to rise together into the light. No man, woman, or child should be left behind on this journey of transformation which humanity is going through right now.

Some of you believe that there is a separation occurring, a separation of light and dark because you see so much chaos, destruction, and death on the planet. But it does not have to be this way, dear ones. There needn't be a separation.

Hold the highest, purest vision that all, and we repeat all, will be delivered into the light. All will rise together into the light.

Those furthest from the god-head, who are causing death and destruction, they too will rise enough to where they will stop inflicting unnecessary harm onto others.

Come together, dear ones, in sacred circle with one another. Pray together and hold a vision for hope, love, and light for everybody on this planet, especially for the leaders who are still in the darkness. We speak of just a select few who are causing death and destruction on the planet. They needn't be eradicated. This is a thought that many of you have: "We just need to get rid of them. We need to expel them from the planet." This is one option, and it could be that some governments choose to do this.

Right now, what we ask from all of you is to gather in a circle at the sacred retreats which you will host in your homes. Imagine and hold a strong vision of everyone and everybody rising enough in vibration, rising enough in consciousness, to where there are no more big wars on the planet. To where there is more peace, harmony, and understanding. To where people come together to work out their differences in a space of love, compassion, and understanding. This is still possible for humanity; this vision that we speak of is still possible.

Some of you don't believe it. You say, "no, the world has fallen too far into darkness." But please, hear our words and know that they are true because they come straight from the god-head, the source of all of creation, directly to the higher self of the channel, and out of his mouth for you to hear. There needn't be too much more death and destruction on the planet; you can come together and work things out in harmony.

This goes for your interpersonal relationships as well, dear ones. For there is a lot of stuff coming up right now between men and women, yes? Especially in regards to intimate, personal relationships, both between friends and lovers. Many of you know what we are speaking of because you are going through it in your relationships with your partners, some of whom you have known for many years. Stuff is coming up to be healed. Be brave, dear ones. Rather than pushing each other away and fighting with each other, come together instead.

Be strong, courageous, brave, and bold in the name of love so that healing can occur on this planet, both interpersonally and collectively.

For every time you heal a relationship between two people, you help bring healing to the collective as well.

Every transmission in this book is of great importance, dear ones. But please know that this one is of particular significance and importance, for it is speaking to this very specific time period that we are in right now. Many of our other teachings are applicable for any time period. But this particular teaching is very relevant for today and for this moment in which you find yourself on planet Earth.

There are many different directions this planet will go in right now. The future is not preordained. It is not pre-written. You are the ones who will choose your own future and each of you has a big contribution to make. This contribution occurs when you meditate every day for long periods of time, rising up into the light and connecting to your own divinity and the god-head where there is love and light for you. And then, when you go out into the world, you share it with others in the best way that you can.

We thank you for listening to this transmission, dear ones, and for taking the time to acknowledge how incredibly important and relevant it is. And so, because this message is of such great importance, we ask that you share it with as many people as possible, for we wish for tens of thousands of people to receive this particular transmission. We are complete, dear ones. Know that you are loved. Many great blessings to you.

STAY OPEN

Chapter 4

Hello, dear ones. We ask you, as you begin to read these words today, to take some very deep breaths, for most of you breathe very shallow breaths. It is necessary to take deeper breaths every now and then. As part of your morning sacred retreat practice, we encourage you to take at least ten, or perhaps even twenty or thirty, deep breaths. Rather than just shallow belly-breathing, the breath *begins* in the belly and then moves into the rib cage and into the heart space to open up space in your heart. Then take a brief pause at the top as you feel your shoulders lift a little bit, slowly exhaling in the opposite direction. This deep breathing will both calm the nervous system *and* energize the body. And this deep breathing will also help to focus the mind, to bring it to a one-pointed focus, which is very helpful for the practice of sacred retreat. So begin this way every day, with these deep breaths.

The channel is continuing to learn how to navigate the experience of being a human being on this planet. For it is not easy all the time, is it? Often challenges arise that must be met with courage and a willingness to learn and grow.

There are two types of people in the world, dear ones. There are the people who will say, "I got it wrong" and they will stay stuck in that energy of regret and self-judgment for months, years, perhaps even an entire lifetime. That is no way to spend a life.

The second type of person which we are encouraging you and the channel to be, is the person who understands that there will often be experiences in life through which you can learn and grow, so that you may move on to the experiences in life that your heart would like to have.

So if you are one of those who is sitting in judgment or regret, we encourage you to *accept* whatever has transpired in your life without judgment, and even with gratitude.

> *For every experience is meant to take you to the next.*
> *And whatever learning and growth has occurred will*
> *certainly bear fruit in the future.*

And so *this,* dear ones, brings us back into this *present* moment in which you are free from the past. You are present, ready, hopeful, and excited for the future.

Things are moving very quickly on the planet right now, dear ones. There is an acceleration that is occurring. And so the lessons are coming more quickly. And so some of you may have the sense that life is becoming *more* challenging. But if you are to face all of the experiences you are having with trust, faith, and courage, then you *will* make it to the other side. And you will look back with the awareness that everything that happened, happened for your greatest good. Because you will step into, and are already stepping into, a new moment and complete alignment with your soul, which is nothing less than the magnificence of god.

Even if it feels like a bumpy ride sometimes, trust that grace is upon you, dearest ones, and that the best is yet to come. For it is. For we see many of you coming out of a long, dark tunnel where there have been trials and tribulations, and into the light where there is more joy, more laughter, more ease, and as we just shared, a greater alignment with your soul, with your spirit that is of god.

So dear ones, celebrate all you have been through. Celebrate where you are. Celebrate what's to come. Celebrate it all.

We know that is a hard thing for most of you to do, to celebrate it all, all of life's experiences. But imagine if you could, dear ones? Imagine if you could truly celebrate all of it. Embrace it all. Not judge anything as being good or bad. But embrace it all. And trust in the victories that are ahead. Trust in the relationships that are coming– the friendships and the romantic partnerships that many of you have been calling for so eagerly in your life. Trust in your abilities to take your gifts and to share them with others in a way that helps you to feel empowered and victorious. For you are molding the clay. And even the unpleasant experiences in life are helping you to mold it in the way that your heart would like to experience life.

Stay open, dear ones. This will be the title of this transmission: "Stay Open." We speak these words because earlier, we were sharing with the channel in his meditation that for some, there is hardening that occurs as one grows older. The channel is approaching fifty years on the planet. And we were sharing with him that it is only natural that he has become a little hardened due to some past experiences in life, some past hurts, that have caused him to become unnecessarily protective and guarded. Which, in turn, prevent him from experiencing life as it is, from *receiving* all that life wants to give him. For perhaps, unconsciously, he pushes some of it away, some of the good stuff. Or he is simply not alert or open to it when it's in front of him. Some of you do the same.

Simply, dear ones, carry with you a subtle intention to be open, to not interpret new situations based on what has occurred in the past. For every new situation is indeed a new situation; a new person, a new opportunity. So be open to it being new rather than allowing what has occurred in the *past* to act as a filter through which you are unable to see the present clearly. In other words, dear ones, be free! Be free from the past – and even be free from the future! From thinking something has to play out in a certain way. Be free from overplanning, for life is meant to happen spontaneously moment to moment. Life is not for planning. It is for *being*.

For what it is most of you seek, is freedom. Freedom to simply be who you are in the moment. To express yourselves freely. And to receive openly and freely.

And so it is, dear ones, that if you feel stuck in a particular pattern, if you are in agreement that some hardening has taken place for you over the years, ask yourself what would help you to get unstuck. Perhaps you need to take a trip somewhere. Put yourself in a new environment where there are less plans. Where you are not thinking and acting so much out of habit, but rather simply being open and free in the present moment.

There is much love for you here, dear ones. Some of you are unable to feel it at this moment because of the hardening that has taken place. Or because your attention has been focused on a challenge in your life. But we want you to know that you are loved. Right here and right now in this moment, you are loved. And so it is dear ones, we want you to take time now to sit, and to simply be open and free.

- Relax
- Allow
- Invite
- Trust

You are loved. And you are love itself.

If somebody were to ask you who you are, the most accurate answer would *not* be to say I am so and so with this name, and this sex, and this job, and these beliefs, these likes, and these dislikes. But rather to say, "I AM loved. I AM love itself." And in fact dear ones, these words are so incredibly powerful, that you might carry them with you as an affirmation of truth:

I AM loved. I AM love itself.
I AM loved. I AM love itself.
I AM loved. I AM love itself.

We feel like this is a wonderful time to seal this transmission. Again we ask you, dear ones, to sit and to *allow* yourself to be loved. For there is *so* much love that is had for you. Love from god, which the channel often refers to as the "supreme creator," who resides outside of creation and as part of creation; love from the divine mother in all of her forms; and love from mother nature and Mother Earth. And of course, love from your pets and from your human companions. There is much love to be had and received here on the planet. We are now complete. Om Shanti. Blessings.

ALIGNING WITH GOD

Chapter 5

There is a shift, friends, that happens when you align yourself with that which you call god. We are going to be quite direct. When you stop being selfish, when you stop trying to satisfy yourself, and begin to live a life of purposeful service, then that which you call god will walk along with you side by side, hand in hand. You will even begin to feel his-her presence in a much more tangible way.

For that is what happens when you move into alignment with your purpose on the planet to live a life of service. And then friends, if it is your intention to live a life of service, if you are taking steps to move forward in that direction, to be of service in a purposeful way, then god will take steps with you. And he-she will provide for you as needed. Miracles will unexpectedly appear in your life to support you. And all that you need to do is to focus on the day at hand without much worry or concern about tomorrow. We say let god take care of tomorrow and you take care of today! Yes?

Meaning, you simply do what you can today to live your life in a purposeful way for all of humanity, to utilize the gifts that creator has given you to be of service.

It is that simple, friends. It is not brain surgery! And then you will be provided for unexpectedly. What you need will show up. This is what happens, friends, when you align yourself with god.

The channel is beginning to feel it now. Even if what he says he needs is not appearing right in front of him in the present moment, he is beginning to have faith that because he becomes more aligned with god every day, that he will be supported. And he will. You know when you are aligned, friends, because you feel it, and you know it. You no longer question, "am I aligned or am I not?" because you know you are. You know that you are aligned with the source that is within you and the source that has created you, and that you are being guided forward for the purpose of being of service on this planet. And certainly, friends, you can have fun while you do it. It was actually meant to be this way. We will say it like this: serving god does not have to be such serious work. It can be fun. It can be joyful. It can be uplifting. And in fact, we would say it is all of these things.

If you are not feeling aligned today, then simply ask yourself some questions: What is one thing I can do today to bring myself into alignment? Who is the one person I can call to offer some support to? Who is the one person I can feed to nourish? Who is the one person I can offer an article of clothing to so they can keep warm? Who is the one person I can give water to because they are thirsty? Who is the one person I can talk to that people often ignore who is in need of some love?

It does not take much to start to move into alignment
with your greatest purpose.

That one step forward will create space and momentum and will bring you into complete alignment with your soul purpose, which is to be of service during this great awakening happening for all of humanity. We said earlier, friends, that your greatest purpose is to live in joy. This is true. It is also your greatest purpose to be in alignment with that which god wants for you.

We will leave you with words that an Indian saint once spoke, a person the channel is very fond of. He said, "Love everyone. Serve everyone." If you are utilizing your gifts to do that, then you are in alignment and you will be taken care of because of it. And you will begin to know that you will be taken care of. There will be much less worry, much less concern, and a lot more faith because you will feel god's presence within you and beside you. And you will know that you are supported in that way.

This is an important teaching, friends. Do not skip over it because your ego says that "it does not apply to me." It applies to all. Do not skip over it, friends, because there is a part of your mind that says it sounds like religious doctrine. It is not.

There is only one true religion, friends, and that is love.
And this teaching comes from that space.

And this was what was at the heart of every religion in its infancy. And we say that it is still present, this truth, in some sects of religion which exist today. In some, it has been tarnished and the truth no longer reveals itself in the religion. But in others, it is still present.

We are going to leave you with that, friends. There is more that we could say about it, but the channel wishes this to be a short teaching.

And you have enough wisdom within yourselves to go a little deeper if you so choose with the words we have left you with, yes? Be of service, friends. Be of service to the one god that we are all part of. And in that way you will be supported. Many of you, the channel himself included, are fond of quotes and affirmations that inspire, yes? And so if you were to put one in front of you today, and every day, let it simply say, "Stay Aligned." And sit with it until you truly get it, until it truly inspires you to move in the direction that you are meant to move in. Blessings, friends.

THE AWAKENING OF JOY
Chapter 6

Good morning, friends. You may say that you are searching for "this" or searching for "that." You may say that you wish to have "this experience" or "that experience". But we say that what you are really seeking is the joy that is within you. And we say that even if you are seeking another to spend time with, in friendship or in romance, that you are still seeking this, an experience of the joy that is within you. It is a joy that is experienced in your heart or in your spirit, simply because this is where joy is experienced, is it not? It is not experienced in your toes (we are making a joke). But perhaps it might be if someone tickles them the right way and you laugh, and the joy within you is awakened.

So, friends, always be clear about what it is you are seeking through all that you do, yes? And if it happens that you wake up and say, "I am not experiencing enough of the joy that I know is within me," then we ask you to sit and to ask yourself what is needed in the moment that will support you and your desire to experience more of the joy that is within you. For what it is today may be very different from what it will be tomorrow or what it was yesterday. Do you see?

But in every moment your spirit will guide you towards
what you need to do to experience more of it.

And so it could be, friends, that you need to release the energy obstructing the joy found within you, yes? And then you may consciously choose how to release this energy. It could be, for example as the channel did a couple of mornings ago, that you go for a run and you make sounds as you do so. And you make other movements with your body that help you to release whatever it is that is preventing you from experiencing the joy that is within you in that moment.

And then at the very least, you will notice a subtle change, a subtle
shift, that brings you a little bit closer to the joy that is within you.
And know that even a very little shift is a shift in the right direction.

On another day, friends, it could be that you simply need to sit with the intention of raising your vibration, with the intention of settling into yourself. And by doing that, you experience more of your essential nature which is joy, yes? Or it could be that you need to push yourself to do something fun, a little outside of the box, something that is a bit uncomfortable for you because it makes you self-conscious. And then you do that, and you feel a little more liberated than you did prior. And you feel a little more joyful. Or if you are an artist as the channel is, it could be that you create joyful art (as opposed to the kind that some are normally acclimated to creating)!

And remember, friends, that there are always people around you who are available to offer you support. So if you sit, and your spirit tells you that it is time to release whatever it is you might label it – a blockage, an obstruction, a filter – and you feel you would be better supported to do that in the presence of another, then do that. In particular, we are speaking of the healers who are available to support you.

And know, friends, that no matter how much joy you are feeling, or how much joy you are not feeling, there is never anything that is wrong with you. You are simply on a journey of awakening, as all of humanity is. You are awakening to that which is within you.

We are going to leave you with this: The essential practice for awakening the joy that is within you is to sit for long enough so that the joy within you has an opportunity to surface, to arise, to awaken.

And if you sit for long enough, in a disciplined way, meaning you do not do it once a week, but rather every day, you will indeed notice the shift that occurs as your true self begins to reveal itself to you. And thus, your vibration will rise. And by way of that, will you experience more of your true self. And you will also experience more synchronicity in your life, as those who are a vibrational match for your new high vibration begin to pop into your life more often. We have great love for you, for all of you. Blessings.

PRACTICE & REFLECT WITH DARREN

Longer Retreats

Hi friends, it's Darren, the channel and author. As noted in Chapter 2, I will be sprinkling some additional practices into appropriate places throughout the book. These practices come from my own life, accumulated over many years, and have served me well. As you read on, you will notice that some of the additional practices I mention are also mentioned by the guides, which means they are very important!

Fifteen to twenty minutes of sacred retreat twice a day is better than nothing; it's a great start. But if you want to get more out of your practice, you will soon need to sit for longer periods of time. As I believe the guides refer to at some point in this book, "the pearl lies at the bottom of the ocean. You have to dive deep to get it." In the shorter sacred retreats, you will start to sink beneath the surface of the ocean (your restless thoughts and emotions). But to get to the pearls on the bottom, you'll need to sit for longer periods of time.

What are the pearls? Just to name a few:

- Deep relaxation: In this fast-paced world, we always think we need to be getting somewhere. But often what we really need is to relax!
- Deep inner-peace that radiates from within yourself: The peace you experience in a deep sacred retreat is beyond any sense of peace you could ever experience in the outside world.
- Intuitive insights: In deeper states of sacred retreat, your intuition blossoms and will guide you forward, helping you to make better decisions, which will lead to a more enjoyable experience of life.

The practice:

At least once a week, carve out two hours of time for sacred retreat in the morning. Be disciplined about this. After one hour, get up and do several half sun salutations for five minutes to energize the body and focus the mind. Then sit back down again for another hour of sacred retreat.

LOVE BEYOND IMAGINATION

Chapter 7

What you are seeking, friends, is within you. Many of you look around you for what it is you are seeking. You seek to find your happiness, and your joy, and your satisfaction in what is labeled as the "outside world." And yet, there is a world that is contained within you that is even more beautiful than what is outside of you. And what you will find within you will be much more satisfactory to you than what you find outside of yourself.

You might say, how can that be? Well, dear ones, are you not in agreement, that no matter what experience you have outside of yourself, no matter how grand it is, that it will pass, yes? It will come. It will go.

But what is contained within you, friends, this will never go.
It will never disappear. We are speaking of the great love
and the great light that is within you.

Dear ones, the very first thing that should be taught to your children is how to go within, how to sit in the stillness of the heart and discover the love and the light inside of themselves. When you find that, friends, everything changes. All of the highs and the lows that you experience in life can be taken light-heartedly because you have discovered what is within yourself. Every great teacher, friends, whom has ever graced their presence on this planet has, in one way or another, spoken these two words: Go Within. It is there that you will find what you are looking for.

So whatever it is you are looking for, friends – be it peace, be it love, be it abundance, be it an experience of joy – you must first go within to find it. You cannot experience it outside of yourself for a prolonged period of time until you have experienced it within yourself. It is just not possible. But once you have discovered it within yourself, you will see and experience much more grace and ease while you are participating in the outside world. And you will be much less attached to all which comes and goes in your life… because you will see it for what it is, which is like a movie that is being played out on the screen of your consciousness.

We say, friends, wouldn't you much prefer to go to the theater and see a good movie versus a bad one? Then it is imperative that you take the time to go within.

Sit in the stillness of your heart, friends. It is there that you will find what you are looking for. It is not outside of yourself.

This world in which you are living is complete with an endless array of distractions that would like to pull you away from your true self. It is like an endless array of advertisements saying, "look at me, look at me, look at me." You need to unplug from all of this, friends. For in the end you will discover that all of these distractions are of very little importance. The only importance, from our perspective, is going within and discovering that there is love within you which is beyond anything you have ever imagined, and that there is love *for* you which is beyond anything that you could have ever imagined.

As more and more people awaken to what is within themselves,
this planet that you are living on will be transformed completely.
You will not even recognize it anymore.

When all have awakened to the love that is within them and take inspired action in the world because they have discovered what is within them, then all will change.

And this shift that we speak of, friends, it is not happening tomorrow. It is happening now. This great shift of consciousness, this great awakening, this great transformation that has been prophesied, is happening now. You are a part of it. Celebrate it! It is a joyous occasion, friends. It is a joyous occasion to be participating in a shift of consciousness of this magnitude occurring on the planet right now. It is of such magnitude that it has never occurred in this way in the history of your planet. The history that we speak of, is the history that you are aware of. There were histories prior to that. But for your civilization, there has never been a time like this. You may say this is history rewriting itself.

It is quite amazing, friends, what is happening on the planet.

The love that is awakening within you, and within all, will touch every nook and cranny of this planet. Nothing will go untouched. And thus, all will be transformed. We know that from your perspective, you would like to see this transformation happen in twenty-four to forty-eight hours! It cannot happen this way. There must be a process or a journey, if you want to call it that, which occurs for this transformation to fully manifest. And during this transformation, you may see that some darkness is becoming visible because more light is being shined upon it. And it is only by way of this light that it is becoming visible. So celebrate that, friends! Celebrate the darkness that is surfacing to be transformed into the light. What we are saying, friends, is that the progress that you seek, if you are what you might label as an "old soul" or a "lightworker," may not happen in your time, meaning the time in which your mind would like to see it occur. But it will happen. It is happening.

The great shift of consciousness of humanity is occurring now.

It is impossible to ignore. Most of all you can sense there is something going on! There is something historic that is occurring on the planet. So again, we tell you to celebrate it. It is a reason to celebrate. Be devoted, friends. If you are going to devote yourselves to something, devote yourselves to unplugging from what it is you need to unplug from. And devote yourself to spending an adequate amount of time every day, preferably every morning and every evening, to go within and to sit in the stillness of your heart. For it is there that you discover who it is you truly are. For it is there that you discover the peace that you truly seek. For it is there that you seek the joy that you wish to experience. For it is there that you experience the love that you have been craving so desperately in your lives. For it is there that you discover the love had for you, which is beyond measure. This is where you discover it all, friends.

Then you open your eyes, and re-engage with the outside world in a way that you hadn't before. You see things differently. You experience things differently. You know yourself differently. You have a greater sense of who it is you are, your place in the world, and what you are meant to be doing in it.

And then do not be afraid, friends, to live the new truth that you have discovered within yourselves, to take the steps that are necessary to live your truth in the world. But it happens by going within first, friends.

The change that you are seeking will not happen by simply chipping away at it, or working hard, or however else you may label it. It happens by going within, discovering, reawakening to, and remembering, all that is within yourself. And then, and only then, sticking your head back out of the turtle's shell and re-engaging with the world, friends. This is a process. It must happen every day, over and over again. In and out, in and out, in and out, until you have been completely transformed, until you look in the mirror and know that you are no longer the same person today that you were prior.

This has already happened for the channel. He has experienced a great shift in consciousness by way of his spiritual practice. He is no longer the same person that he was even just a few years ago. He may look more or less the same, yes? He may have the same hair color, the same eyes, the same sense of humor, some of the same quirks, and maybe even some of the same tendencies that he is still working out. But as a whole, he is a completely different person. It is as if he has been reborn. And he will be reborn again, and perhaps again, all in this one incarnation, as he continues to elevate himself, to raise his vibration, and to experience this great shift of consciousness that is happening on the planet right now and that is being supported by mother earth, who is also raising her frequency.

And so it is, you too, friends, are experiencing this great shift of consciousness. You too, friends, if you have not already, will soon realize that you are no longer the same person that you were prior.

You will soon realize that you too have been reborn.
That is exciting, is it not?

Perhaps you believed that you only get one birth. But it is not this way in this incarnation, friends. You are being reborn over and over and over again, all of you. By going within, by way of the alchemical process that occurs, and by way of your spiritual practice.

We celebrate all of you, friends. We celebrate all of you for the journey you are on. You are brave souls. That is who you are. Continue to do the work you are doing. Continue to go within. Continue to transform yourself. And thus you will transform the world.

Do not be afraid to go within anytime, any place, whenever you feel a pull from something outside of yourself that wants to distract you from what is important. That is the time to close your eyes, to go within, and to sit in the stillness of your heart. Of course, we do not want you to do this while you are driving a motor vehicle or while you are walking down the street because we do not want you to bump into people! But we want you to do this often, even if it is just for a few minutes, in addition to your morning and evening practice. Close your eyes. Go within. Honor the truth that is within you by doing so.

Do not be afraid about what other people will think. If nothing else, friends, you will spark their curiosity. They will want to know what it is you've got that they don't. Because they will see you with your eyes closed. They will see you meditating, or going within, or whatever else it is you wish to call it. They will see a gentle smile on your face. They will even see a glow to your heart.

They will feel a particular energy or a particular frequency radiating from your heart, through your energy field, and out into the world.

Perhaps they will want to sit close to you and get a little taste of it. And most certainly they will be inspired to try it for themselves. At first, as it was for you, friends, it may be a little bit of a struggle for them, yes? Because, as you know, sacred retreat, stilling the mind, experiencing the bliss that is within you, may not come easily at first. But with practice, it does come.

And so, support your friends. Tell them, "It was difficult for me at first as well. I too wanted at times, to give up on the practice. But I stuck to it. And because of that, my life has changed. Now my mind is still most of the time. More often than not, I reside in a state of equanimity, meaning the highs and lows that occur outside of myself do not move me as much as they used to. I am more loving. I am more compassionate. I am kinder to strangers. I receive more intuitively than I used to. I feel like I am being guided from a higher power that is within myself. I feel that I am supported. I feel that I am loved. I have a greater sense of knowing of myself as spirit. I know that I am much more than this particular person who has a name, a job, and a place to live. I know I am a multidimensional being who can draw upon countless incarnations of experience in the incarnation that I find myself in now." Perhaps you will not say *all* of this to your friends. But you will say what is appropriate for each of them individually. You get where we are going with this, yes?

We will leave you with this, friends. Through your spiritual practice, you will come to experience this shift of consciousness that we are speaking of, if you have not already. And then you are to reach out your hand and show others how to do it as well. And you can do that by being an example in the world and by not being afraid to display your practice for all to see. Not because you have an ego and you want to receive gratification in that way but simply because it is your truth, to follow your inner guidance, and to go within whenever you please. That is it for today, friends. Blessings. Or as the channel says when he teaches yoga, "Namaste!" The light in us sees the light in you.

THE TRUE PURPOSE OF MEDITATION

Chapter 8

Good morning, friends. There are many good reasons to cultivate a practice of sacred retreat. Yet, in the way that meditation is advertised to you today, seldom is the true purpose of the practice revealed. And so it is, friends, that we wish to take a few minutes this morning to remind you of the real reason for meditation (as the channel calls it) for the practice of sacred retreat (as we call it).

The practice of sacred retreat is the gift that is given to you by your creator so you can know yourself.

And we are not talking of the self that you normally think of when we utilize that word. But rather the true self. Perhaps, friends, the true self is something that you cannot see. But it is certainly something that you can feel. You may look in the mirror and say to yourself, "Oh, that is myself!" But no, it is not. That is your physical form. And so it is, the practice of sacred retreat has been gifted to you so that you may know your true self.

We are going to put it quite simply. The nature of your true self is bliss. And so, it is unlikely that you will sit down for just one practice of sacred retreat and come to know your true self! It is unlikely you will sit down once and come to know yourself as bliss.

But we tell you this, friends, there is nothing more important in life than discovering your true self. There is nothing more important than having a direct experience of it.

And it is not in spite of all that you are doing in the outside world. In actuality, the discovery of your true self will enable you to have a much more pleasurable life experience. And so as we always do, friends, we draw you back to the essential teaching of this book, which is to sit and to allow the bliss of your own being to reveal itself to you. And it will, little by little. Be patient with yourselves, friends.

When you sit, sit without expectation. Sit softly. Allow yourself to relax deeply. Allow yourself to become receptive. Allow yourself to let go of that which is happening around you, so that you can experience what is happening within you, in the place where your spirit resides. And there you shall find who it is you are, yes? There you shall access the true self. For most of you, friends, this will be revealed to you little by little, over a long period of time. But we tell you that your devotion, your commitment, and we will even say your *discipline*, will be rewarded by way of the experience that you have. So it is, so shall it be. Blessings, friends.

PRACTICE & REFLECT WITH DARREN

Daily Rituals

Personally, daily rituals that support my practice of sacred retreat have become incredibly valuable. What comes before and after sacred retreat is almost as important as the sacred retreat itself. So here's some guidance that you may find useful for your practice.

- When you get out of bed, go straight to your meditation chair. Do not check your cell phone, do not turn on your laptop, and do not do anything else besides going directly to your chair. Be very disciplined about this.

- After your sacred retreat, I lovingly encourage you to have a slow, mindful morning before entering the "real world." Make a healthy breakfast. Drink at least two cups of water or green juice. Eat mindfully and slowly. Don't multitask; in other words, don't eat your breakfast while checking your email!

- Feel free to add anything else to your morning routine that feels good to you. Only after your routine should you plug in your router, check your phone, and check your email. If you need to go to bed one hour earlier in order to get up one hour earlier and have this sacred time for yourself, then do that.

- In the evening, follow a similar routine. Turn everything off before you sit for sacred retreat. Set a strict time to do this. For me, it's 9pm at the very latest but usually 8pm. If it helps you to relax, you can include some spiritual reading before or after your sacred retreat. Spiritual reading could be a chapter of this book. But it could also be any other holy text that feels uplifting and inspiring to your spirit.

RETURNING TO BALANCE

Chapter 9

From our heart to your heart, we greet you with great love. And we greet you with admiration as well! For what a great gift it is to be present during this time of awakening and to be experiencing a human incarnation. This is the place to be!

Perhaps some of you, like the channel, used to go to clubs. And you would want to go to the one that was most popular, the one with the longest line, the one that was most exclusive. Well, my friends, you are already there! Earth is the place to be. For this is where the great awakening is taking place. And while certainly it is taking place in many different dimensions and in many different star systems, we will tell you that where you are, is exactly where you have chosen to be.

And if your mind reacts to this by saying, "I am not where I want to be in my life," let that thought go. That thought will only serve to create resistance. Instead, open up to the beauty and the possibility that is inherent in this ever-expanding present moment in which you find yourself. The present moment, my friends, is the only place to be. And again we reiterate, this is why every great spiritual teacher has always included the word "presence" in his or her teachings.

Some of you might be surprised that we say "his or her." There have been many great female spiritual teachers on this planet as well as males. Though they might not be as well known as some of the male spiritual teachers who come to mind while we say these words, these women were also incredibly powerful teachers of the light. So now is the time on your planet to honor and respect the divine masculine and the divine feminine.

The channel is sitting waiting for us to transmit the next teaching and becoming a little bit impatient. But he has only been sitting for a few minutes! We laugh! And so, we use this example as a reminder to tell you, it is perfectly okay to sit, and to do what you label as "nothing." And to slow down. And to retreat back inside of yourself even if you are not on sacred retreat. You can do this many times during your day. You can do this while you are eating your food, or reading a book, or engaging in any mindful activity that's good for your soul. You can slow down and relax and sit back inside of yourself. We encourage any experience that helps you do this. The channel is thinking of taking a long bath with rose petals. Yes, that would be nice!

You will know when you are there, in that relaxed state of being, because it is a feeling. It is a feeling that everything is perfect and okay in your state of relaxation. And that it is actually more pleasurable than being out there in the rat race. And we know how your mind works. Right away your mind says, "Oh, but I need to be out there in the rat race." We say these moments of deep relaxation are more important. There is a reset that happens during these moments of relaxation. The nervous system relaxes and healing can take place.

As your mind relaxes, your cells can regenerate and
restore you to your divine blueprint.

This can only happen in a state of relaxation. The channel is still waiting. He is saying, "what is the teaching for today?" This is the teaching, friends! We laugh! The teaching is that it is okay to relax.

Much earlier in our conversation we referenced the turtle who sticks his head in and out of his shell. We encourage you to go on sacred retreat twice a day, so that every time you stick your head back out of your shell, your experience of the outside world changes a little bit. You are more absorbed in peace and certainly, you are more connected to the great love that is in your heart.

And so we wish you to extend this teaching of going in and out, this teaching of weaving, into your daily life. Many of you might be familiar with the yin and the yang. The yin is the more passive energy. Passive does not mean disengaged; it simply means that you are in a state of relaxation, that you are not trying to do anything. The yang is the more fiery aspect which has you out in the world choosing to put your attention to things that serve your purpose, we hope.

Many of you are out of balance. And it is not enough to simply go on your sacred retreat twice a day. You must find a balance of these yin and yang energies. If you look at the yin-yang symbol, you will see that both sides are equal in size. This is for good reason! The yang does not take up more space than the yin. They are in perfect balance.

They are in perfect harmony. And we are asking you to seek out the same balance in your life.

Find the balance between the yin and the yang.

Find the balance between activities that help you relax and help you sit back inside of yourself, and activities that you consider to be work. The channel is thinking of some European countries that allow people to have very long afternoon naps. This is a good example of finding the balance between the yin and the yang. Again, we see many of you thinking, "Well, this is good in theory. We do not disagree with you. But I don't have the time." To you we say that it is okay to start small. Even if it is scheduling ten to fifteen minutes of time, two or three times a week, to do something that helps you relax, that is a good start. And once you are in the flow of doing that, you might very well feel inspired to create more time for relaxation, to come back into balance, to come back into harmony. And some of you, as you begin to embody this particular teaching of ours, might have the awareness that you wish to make changes in your life which allow you to have more of this relaxation time. Some of you might even be inspired to live simpler lives, which do not require as much money, but bring greater levels of peace and thus, great contentment.

The channel teaches yoga. There is a pose in the practice of yoga called "child's pose". And this pose is the one that you take when you want to relax and do nothing. Ideally, we would like to see you taking an equal amount of child's poses as you do the poses that require effort and exertion. It is all about balance, my friends.

You need to bring yourselves back into balance if you are out of it.
And then you will see that mysteriously, you begin to feel better.

Do not be afraid, dear ones, to break the rules in order to find this balance that we speak of. You have the right to subscribe to the rules of society which resonate with you. And for those of you who are not ready to end your unhealthy subscriptions quite yet, you do not have to subscribe for the rest of your lives! You can begin to make changes that help you create more balance in your lives today.

We are speaking of the rules that keep you busy all of the time, and which do not give you time for relaxation to come into balance, nor to experience this harmony that we speak of. Consider placing a yin-yang symbol somewhere where you can see it quite easily. This will serve as a gentle reminder to seek out moments of relaxation.

And indeed, as the channel is discovering himself to create more space for this, it might be necessary to let go of some things that occupy your time and that are not of necessity. Now is the time for prioritizing, for asking yourself, "What activities are nurturing my soul purpose? What activities are related to fulfilling my soul contract and how can I best be of service in the world?" And then you will see, there are many things you are doing that are wasteful of your time and energy, which are both sacred. And thus, it is quite important to choose wisely how you spend your time and where you put your energy. So that the time that you do have can be devoted to what is of great importance in your life.

If you feel tremendous resistance towards what we have spoken of in this chapter, that is okay. We simply ask you to return to it at a future date. We encourage you to say to yourself, "Okay, I will read this chapter again next season, in a few months from now. And perhaps then, I will feel less resistance." Many blessings, friends. Know that we are with you always, that you have our great love and our great support as you take this sacred journey.

HUMANITY IS WAITING FOR YOU

Chapter 10

Hello, friends. Today we are going to talk about fear. From the very beginning of time, fear has been part of your consciousness, has it not? From the moment of your separation from that which you call your "father" or your "mother" god, the ego and the physical body itself produced what you label as "fear."

Most of you though, when you look around you, notice that there is not much to be fearful of anymore, is there? What we mean is that in this particular moment, it is likely that you feel quite safe – you are not afraid that there are lions, tigers, or bears outside of your home waiting to attack you! You are not afraid that your neighboring tribe is going to surprise you in the middle of the night with a sneak attack! If you happen to be one who is reading these words and is in one of those situations, then it is time to pray. We are not joking. It is time to pray for your safety and that all will be done for the greatest good for yourself and all of humanity.

But perhaps you are like the channel, sitting comfortably in his home with what we are going to label as "normal everyday concerns." And you know in your heart and in your spirit, that there are steps to be taken to fulfill your purpose here on this planet outside of your sacred retreat practice. And perhaps, like the channel, you feel fear because you are worried that it might not go well, or up to the expectations of your ego. You are worried that you might fail, yes? Perhaps you are even worried that you will be ridiculed!

Well we are going to tell you a secret, friends. Many of you know this to be true already. The greatest successes that have ever occurred on this planet, the greatest triumphs that have ever occurred on this planet, the greatest contributions that were ever made to the upliftment of humanity, were done in the midst of a little bit of fear. Do you see what we are getting at, friends?

If there are steps that you know you need to take in your life, but you are feeling fear around them, we say now is the time to take those steps in spite of this fear, friends.

If you are not going to do it now, then when are you going to do it? Are you going to do it tomorrow? You might say yes but then something will come up tomorrow, yes? And you will say, "Oh well, today is not the day. So I will do it tomorrow." And then you might say the same thing over and over again. And then it is over, yes? Then you leave your physical form and perhaps you come back again in a different form. And you get another go at fulfilling your purpose.

We say, why not fulfill it now? The time is ripe to do so for all of you. No matter what your individual purposes are, now is the time to do it. The channel is saying, "I do not know if I am ready to channel for more people publicly." And we are telling him, "Yes you are." We are telling him that. We are telling him, like everything else he has ever done in his life, that he will learn as he goes along! It will not be perfect right away. It is not expected to be so. But you must start somewhere, yes?

With everything else in his life, he is making great progress because he is simply taking it step by step. He is tuning into what is required in the present moment for each of his many projects. And he is doing what is required for each of those projects! He is doing so not by pushing and not by forcing the matter, but by listening and taking action when he knows it is time to take action, when spirit is leading him to do so. And very often, this inspired action comes out of silence. It comes from the time that is taken in sacred retreat, time in which he becomes receptive to the guidance that his spirit has for him. We are offering you this as a friendly reminder that none of what we are saying now detracts from anything else we have said prior to this teaching. It all goes hand in hand, yes? They are all spokes on the wheel of your spiritual practice and your purpose for being here on the planet.

What we are saying, friends, is that if you know in your heart that now is the time for action, then take it, just as we are telling the channel to do.

Take that step forward, yes? And keep taking the steps.

If you do that, friends, then one day in the not-too-distant future, you will be on top of the mountain. And you will have only gotten there because you took it step by step, yes? Do you see what we mean? You will not have to put on a cape like superman and fly to the top of the mountain! No, not in the bodies you are in right now.

It is likely that on the way you will meet people who will help pull you up to the next step! We want you to know that we see all these people ahead of you. They are waiting for you to take the next step. Do you see what we mean by that? They can only greet you, they can only help you, they can only help lift you up to the next one, if you arrive where they are. So you must take that first initial step to greet them, friends. And we tell you, that if you do that, your helpers will arrive. They will be there in time – at the perfect time, in fact. And you will receive all that you need to continue on with the journey to climb to the top of the mountain.

This, the top of the mountain, is your purpose being expressed in the world, friends. This is the top of the mountain that we speak of. It is the time in your life when you are contributing to the great awakening that is happening on the planet, to the best of your capabilities. So we say, why not keep climbing, why not keep taking the steps? This is it, friends. This is the motivational chapter where we become your life coaches and we say, "You can do it. Yes you can!" Because it is required for many of you, friends, yes?

The spiritual practice always comes first, friends. It must. Without it, there is nothing at all.

This we are quite adamant about. Once you have understood that, then you are free and liberated to take the steps that you need to take to fulfill your purpose on the planet. And once you have become receptive by way of your spiritual practice, you will be led. You will no longer be taking steps that are blind. Do you see what we mean by that, friends?

It is the mind that so often takes misdirected steps simply because it thinks it must take action. But the action that we are telling you to take is a different kind of action, yes? It comes from within. It comes from your spirit that guides you forward. And so it is, you must become receptive to your spirit by way of your spiritual practice. And then when the time is ripe, you must take each step with great faith in what is not seen ahead of you. You must have faith in yourself, friends. You must have faith that your helpers will arrive when they are needed, that you will be uplifted in the perfect time and at the perfect place to the next step, until you reach the top.

We have often told you, in many ways, that there is nowhere to really get to, yes? And so when you are on the top of the mountain, friends, and let's say for now that it is in what we would label as "future timeline," in this incarnation that you find yourself, you will know three things. Number one, you will know that you have become all of yourself, that you are fully embodied with the god-presence that is already within you. And number two, that you are now fully expressing that god-presence in the world and thus contributing in every way possible to the great awakening that is occurring for all of humanity.

Yet at the same time, you will know by way of direct experience, that there never was, there never is, and there will never be any place to get to. It is not meant to be a riddle, friends. Many of you get it. You will know that, friends, because by way of direct experience you will be one with mother-father god. This is what you might call the zenith of your spiritual climb, or better to say your "spiritual ascent," through the clouds to the very top of the mountain which you are destined to reach in this incarnation. This is of incredible importance.

In fact, we would say that this is what is most important in this particular teaching.

Many are waiting for you. What we mean by that, friends, is that humanity is waiting for you to fulfill your purpose because they need you. They need to be uplifted.

From where you are right now friends, on the mountain, there are many who are much lower than you are. Do not take that as an opportunity to pass judgment or to get back into your ego. It simply means that they are farther away from knowing who they really are. Right now, you are able to help them, simply by way of where you are and where they are. But when you get to the top, friends, you will be able to help many. In fact, we can even say that you will be able to help all. Do you see what we mean by that, friends? Do you see what we mean when we say many are waiting for you? They are waiting for you to fulfill all of the potential that is rising from within you.

We are going to put it another way, friends. You are all light workers, yes? When you reach the top of the mountain, you will be able to shine your light upon all who are making the ascent. And they will all be uplifted by your presence. They will all be uplifted because you are expressing the great love, the great light, and the great truth that is within you. And they will all be uplifted by your presence because your presence will be one with that which you call mother-father god. This is why we say humanity is waiting for you, friends. We do hope this message inspires you to keep climbing, to keep taking the steps that are necessary in your lives, friends.

Life is short, yes? Certainly eternal life, the life of your soul, is not. That is eternal. But life in the mortal form that you are in right now will not go on for eternity. And so again, we encourage you to utilize this incarnation, this human birth, this gift that you have been given by supreme creator, to fulfill your purpose and to know fully the god presence that is within you and that *is* you.

> *The higher you climb, friends, the greater the impact you*
> *have on humanity. The greater the impact you have*
> *on the consciousness of humanity.*

And even if people forget your name after you have gone, it does not matter. For the contribution will have been made, yes? In time, friends, many names will have been forgotten! Even many of the names that you know now. They will be like dust in the wind. But your contribution will still be present. Your love will still be present. The change that you ushered in for this planet will still be present. And so in that way, you will be remembered, honored, and cherished by all of humanity… as spirit.

When you look back upon your endless cycle of incarnations, you will say, "Oh yes, with that particular name, I did that. With that particular name, I did this. Yet no matter what my name was, it was always me who was embodied in all these different forms, contributing in all of these different ways. Oh and yes! Look at that incarnation there, yes. That is the one in which I read the book by The Teachers of The Light. And I found it very inspirational! And so it is that I kept climbing to the top of the mountain. And oh wow, in that particular incarnation, a great many people were uplifted because of the work that I did on the planet." This is what we call "spiritual pride," friends. It does not come from your ego. It comes from your spirit. It is a sense of well-being and worth because of the contribution that you have made.

We will leave you with this, friends. Many of you are making quite a contribution already! In fact, all of you are, in your own way. We remind you that even in the simplest of moments, you are contributing. Never let that go, friends. We are not telling you to lose sight of the present moment, not at all. This (the top of the mountain) is a very specific teaching for very specific moments in your lives, friends, when you are feeling that fear. And it is for when you are iffy as to whether to take that next step. This teaching is for that. So refer to it when you have that kind of moment. Many blessings.

THE GREAT SPIRIT

Chapter 11

This next transmission is from a Native American group of guides, *The Council of Elders*.

Hello, my friends. It is a great honor and a great privilege to speak to you in this way. We are not the light teachers that you have become acclimated to spending time with. We are a different group of teachers. We are teachers of the light too, but we do not call ourselves by that name. We call ourselves *The Great Council of Elders*.

We consist mainly of Native American energies, some of whom the channel has known in other incarnations. We have been given permission from the other light teachers to share some of our knowledge and our wisdom with you.

The Teachers of The Light say this is the time of awakening. This is very true. Many are awakening now on your planet. We say you are awakening to something new and something old at the same time. You are reawakening to the wisdom of your ancestors who walked in harmony with Great Mother Earth.

We did this when we had our incarnations as Native Americans, not out of obligation, but because we felt a deep resonance in our hearts with Great Mother Earth. We saw and experienced that the Great Spirit, the one that you might call god, was present in all of creation. And thus, we honored it, we worshiped it, and we celebrated it. We would like you to do the same because it will make you feel good to reconnect in this sacred way.

The Teachers of The Light have been sharing many practices with you to help you to come into resonance with the heart. We want to share with you our practices which do the same. So, this first practice that we share with you, is to reawaken to The Great Spirit that is within all of god's creation. You must spend some time in nature to do this. There is no other way.

So, pick a day that is convenient for you. And when the day comes, do not make excuses why you cannot go! You will be pleased once you do. And simply sit in nature and observe. Sit in your heart and observe creation and you will see that this god that many speak of is present throughout it. This practice will help you to reconnect to a part of you that has been lost in the modern world.

It is not your fault. You were raised a certain way. And for most of you, it was in a way that was disconnected from the Great Mother. And so now we are asking you to reconnect. And once you do this, your life will be filled with much more meaning because you will feel more connected to what we call The Great Spirit, or what you call god. And thus, you will feel a much deeper connection to the presence of god that is inside of you. You will also feel a much deeper connection to your heart that sits at the center of this god-Presence.

This is the practice we share with you today, my friends. We will be back to share two or three more in this book. And next time we speak to you in this way, we will build the fire a little bit higher. Today we light the fire in your heart with this first practice. And with each of our teachings, the fire will grow higher and higher. And this fire will keep you very warm.

And in time, if you are not doing so yet, many of you will actually gather together in front of this fire and share in community, in the oneness that The Teachers of The Light speak of. This is what we see for you.

So you know, we call you "The Great Warrior Tribe." And when we say "you," we mean the entire human race. You are warriors who are reawakening to the divinity that is within you and all around you. And so we honor you, for the warrior that you are. And know that this warrior extends to both male and female. Many blessings, friends.

BECOMING A CHANNEL

Chapter 12

Good morning, friends! As always, it is a great pleasure to be with you. The channel is learning that, in everything he does, the energy flows more effortlessly if he is in a state of receptivity. And a state of receptivity is what allows energy to flow. If you are not in a state of receptivity, it is kind of like having a dam that is preventing the flow of water. But when you are receptive, you lift up the dam and the energy can flow.

If you are always one step ahead of yourself, thinking of the next thing you need to do, you are not being receptive.

But if your mind is still, and you are present to the moment that is at hand, then you are being receptive. Then you are at least opening yourself up to receptivity. And isn't it true that what you all seek is to receive? You seek to receive inspiration, creative ideas, new people into your lives who stimulate you, and new experiences that delight you! And so to receive, or to call these things into your life, you need to be receptive. And so, this is why learning the art of stilling your mind and being completely present in the moment is the most essential spiritual practice. And then in receptivity, you can be receptive to your heart as well.

So when we speak of weaving in and out of the depths of your heart center, we also speak of weaving in and out of receptivity. And our wish is that you will be receptive as often as possible. If you circle back around to all of our teachings so far, you will see that in one way or another, they are all designed to bring you into a state of receptivity.

In one way or another, you are all channels.

For you are expressing the presence of god that is within you, through you. You are expressing this presence through your eyes, through the words that you speak, and through the vibration of your heart that will inform the words you speak. And of course, your actions will also be informed by the vibration of your heart. And so, you might begin to explore this idea that you too are a channel. If you would like to open yourself up to channeling energies that will change the world and tickle your soul at the same time, then put yourself into a state of receptivity. And if you sit, and you feel blocked, like the dam has not been lifted, that is fine. Sit with the intention of channeling whatever it is you would like to channel consistently. And with this intention, eventually things will begin to flow. And then you will not only be in a state of receptivity, you will be in a state of creativity! And this, my friends, is your natural state of being.

By your very nature, you are creators!

So by stilling your mind, by being present, by being receptive, and by practicing channeling, you are empowering yourself to be who you are, which is a creative being who has unlimited access to the source of your being. The channel is thinking of an antenna coming out of his crown chakra, lifting up into the higher realms. And yes, it is quite like that! When you still your mind, when you move into presence, when you become receptive, and when you commit to sitting as many times as it is needed until the energy begins to flow, you are lifting your antenna and becoming a channel.

So now we ask you, friends, what is it that you would like to channel? For the channel we are transmitting these words through, he channels many different energies. He is a channel for reiki. He is a channel for music. He is a channel for our words. And yet, all of these things, though they might appear separate, come from the same source of unlimited potential and unlimited creativity. It is a source that resides within you and outside of you at the same time. It is indeed everywhere and everything.

Very likely what you would like to channel is related to your soul purpose, your soul contract, your mission! Certainly, everything that the channel is channeling is related to his soul contract, or soul mission. And so friends, you might play around with this idea that we bring to you today: that you are a channel. And that you too can do as the channel is doing! It may not be by speaking out loud the words that are being transmitted from a different group of energies. But it may be in a way that is suitable for you, that takes into account the gifts that you have to share with the world, your soul contract, and your desire to be the creative being that you are.

There is great freedom that is found when you open yourself up to being a channel and expressing yourself in a creative way on this planet. It is like tickling yourself and giving yourself great pleasure.

And we say, why not do that? Why not focus all of your attention, whenever you have free time, on tickling yourself in this way instead of allowing yourself to be distracted by things that do not tickle you.

If you are one of those who is looking down at your phone like a bobble head that never stops moving, we offer you an invitation to focus your energies on tickling yourself in a more pleasurable way.

Express yourselves, dear ones. This is what you are meant to do here on this planet. Express yourselves as the unique individuals that you are.

And as you are doing so, do it in a state of oneness so that you perceive yourself as both separate and one with all of humanity. Open yourself up. Loosen yourself up.

Allow the energy to flow! Do whatever you need to do to get it flowing. Shake your body if you need to. Get the energy moving, yes? The channel knows that when he is in this state of receptivity, and the energy is flowing, he is most content. Then he can leap like a frog, from channeling reiki, to channeling our words, to channeling music. And thus, he experiences himself as the creative being that he is. And even in moments when he is doing things out of obligation, once the energy is flowing, he can quite easily start the flow again when he so desires.

So dear ones, we will leave you with this question: what do you want to be a channel for? Whatever it is, it should both tickle you and should bring light into the world. If it meets those two requirements, then you have our full support. And you will notice, friends, that if it is your intention to sit in your heart center while you are channeling, while you are expressing yourself, while the energy is flowing, you will find it even more delightful. It will tickle your soul even more.

- Do not be shy about bringing your gifts into the world!
- Do not be shy about expressing yourself!
- Do not be shy about sharing the great light that is within you with the entire world.

From our heart to your heart, with great love, we send you off into the world to be a channel for the light, reminding you that you are a great light worker. Blessings.

THE LIGHT BODY

Chapter 13

Good morning, friends. There is an experience of enlightening that is occurring for all on the planet. The channel himself is experiencing a little bit of it today.

His physical body is feeling a little bit unusual. He would be very quick to label it as sick. But we much prefer the word "unusual," meaning it does not feel the way it normally feels. And this is a good thing! It means that he is enlightening. It means that something, and he knows what it is, that he has picked up through his life experience is rising to the surface to be released so that his physical body may become lighter and lighter, until it feels like he is walking on air, even though his feet are very much still touching the ground.

So what we say to you today, friends, is do not fight this process of enlightening. The mind will be very quick to think, "I wish to feel the way I did yesterday. I felt better yesterday." This is just a thought, my friends.

If you are enlightening, you will know it because it will feel
a little bit different than what you label as being "sick"
or being "under the weather."

Do you understand? And rather than fighting it, we encourage you to say, "Yes! I am enlightening! What a great day it is today!" And then trust, my friends, that your body knows what it is doing. And even if it is a little bit uncomfortable for a day, or a few days, or even longer, that the infinite intelligence of your being is helping you to enlighten in the most easeful way.

You can assist this process of enlightening by not resisting it. If you resist it, you will create struggle. It will be like trying to swim upstream. It is a lot easier to go with the flow and to allow the enlightening to occur. The channel is asking us to be a little more specific about this word we are choosing to use, "enlightening." It is simply the release of all that is not truly yours, the release of what is not love. There is no need to hold onto it any longer. Remember, this is the time of the great awakening. And during this time of awakening, you must release and let go of all that is not yours. So let it go.

We encourage you to say these words out loud: "I allow myself to
release, to let go, and to enlighten. I give back what is not mine."

The channel was planning to go to the gym today, to lift weights, to get big and strong! As we often do, we are laughing through the words of the channel. Instead, he is now being led to the park to give back to the Earth and the trees, to recycle this energy that is not his, that he no longer wants, and of which he is ready to let go. If you really give yourself permission to release and let go of what is not yours, this process of enlightening will be quick. It will not last for a very long time. If you resist, if you fight to hold onto what is not yours, your body will tell you, because you will continue to feel unusual.

Some of you might need a little bit of assistance, a little bit of support, as you enlighten. That is fine. Call upon your soul brothers and your soul sisters, who are eager to help you enlighten. The channel is one of those who is very gifted at helping others do this. He does this through reiki and by holding space for light beings to come into his healing room and to support people as they enlighten. So we encourage you to tune in, to listen to your body, and if you are enlightening, allow it to happen. And ask yourself, "What do I truly need to do today to support myself during this enlightenment?" You will know what the answer is, yes?

It could be that you need to take a day or two, or even more, off from your work. It could be that you need to sit and to allow energy to flow down your legs, through your feet, and into The Great Mother Earth to be recycled. It could be that you need to return to The Great Mother, and to sit with her, to sit in the womb of creation. And simply in a state of allowing, she will gladly take what is not yours and recycle it. For she is your mother and she loves all of you greatly. And she will do all that she can to assist in your great awakening, for your awakening is her awakening as well. Together you are awakening and supporting each other.

The channel is thinking of something a teacher said to him one time: "It is much easier to let go than to hold on." And so, that will be our final message for you today.

Do not hold on to what it is you do not need.

Every time you enlighten, your body becomes lighter and lighter, and you have greater access to the great love and the great light that resides within you. And you find yourself rooted to The Great Mother, grounded, resting in your heart center, and with a column of light that extends out from your crown chakra to the higher realms. And thus, you feel as tall as the sky and yet have roots that extend all the way down to the center of The Great Mother. So you might think of yourself as a tree. And your heart center resides right in the space where the branches extend out to touch the hearts and souls of all those whose paths you cross.

We send you our great love and our great support during this process of enlightening that is occurring for all on the planet. As shared earlier, the Native American guides who are close to the channel see the human race as the great warrior tribe. And so they want you to know that you have brought great strength and great courage with you into this incarnation. And it is with this great strength and great courage that you can enlighten gracefully and easefully, with love. Blessings, friends.

PRACTICE & REFLECT WITH DARREN

Mindfulness

One of the many benefits sacred retreat brings into our lives is mindfulness. The word "mindfulness" isn't as it sounds. It doesn't mean living with a full mind! It means being conscious and aware.

In sacred retreat, that's exactly what we are doing. We are being conscious and aware of an "object of awareness," most commonly the breath moving in and out of the nostrils. We are softly but intently focusing our attention on that object of awareness. Doing so helps us cultivate the ability to be highly present with the moment at hand which, in truth, is the only moment that exists.

Sacred retreat becomes even more valuable when we bring our practice into the world with us, into our everyday experience in life. In a heightened state of mindfulness, you can now be more aware of:

- Your thoughts
- Your words
- Your actions
- Where you're placing your attention in every moment of life

When you catch yourself having a thought that doesn't serve you, sit for a short sacred retreat to still your mind or choose to "reframe." A "reframe" is when you choose a healthier, more supportive thought. For example:

Old Thought: I am not good enough.
New Thought: I am worthy of great love in my life.

Our thoughts are incredibly powerful; they help to shape our reality. Our emotional and physical well-being are directly connected to our thoughts. If we think negative thoughts, lower vibrational emotions will follow and soon, the body will start feeling ill as well. So be mindful of your thoughts throughout the day!

Other things to be mindful of:

- The food you put into your body. Choose foods that will truly uplift you and put you in a good mood.
- What you watch on television or online. Choose to watch programming that will truly uplift and inspire you, rather than the "other kind."
- How much attention you give to social media. My general rule of thumb is one time a day for five minutes, max.
- Who you spend time with. Only spend time with people who truly honor and respect you and make you feel uplifted. Being spiritual does not mean you need to forgo healthy boundaries.

In sacred retreat, you are raising your vibration and moving closer to god-source, while god-source is moving closer to you. The higher you get, the more important it becomes to protect and nourish your high vibration. By following the guidance above, you'll "stay high" and have a more enjoyable experience of life.

AWAKENING TO JOY

Chapter 14

Good morning, friends. Many of you have a list of things you need to do to get to where you are going, to get to where you think are meant to be. But friends, are you beginning to see that there is nowhere you really need to be except for in your heart center? For when you are there, you feel complete. You feel whole. You feel at one with your creator. You feel at one with the love that is the very fabric of existence. And that is all you need. And this is why it is likely, on your own accord, without needing us to push you, that you will begin to spend longer periods of time in your sacred retreat. Why? Because it will feel good! It is that simple. And when the mind thinks, "Oh, I must get up and do this or do that," it will then have a more productive thought that says, "No, I need to sit for a longer period of time and sit even deeper into what it is I am beginning to feel in the depths of my own heart."

They do say that all good roads lead to the heart, yes? There are some roads outside of yourself that lead there.

*But if you want to experience the depths of the heart
that we speak of, you must go within.*

And it is there that you will find everything that you are looking for. And then, in this space of the heart, you can go out into the world with great purpose, which is to lead others into their heart centers as well. And once you are reconnected to this purpose for which you are here on this planet, you will begin to make changes that support this purpose.

And here in the higher realms, from which you are not separate, we will celebrate as you embark upon this new way of being! The channel is smiling as he transmits our words. He does so because he sits in his heart. He is thinking of a bumper sticker for a car that says, "When you sit in your heart, you will smile". And we do agree that when you sit in your heart, you will smile. And it will not be forced. It will be the love in your heart that is causing you to smile and causes you to experience joy that rises from within yourself.

Do you see, friends, that the vibration of joy is not one that is sought out? It is not one that can be sought out through outer experience. It is a vibration that arises from within yourself. And as it arises, then you naturally attract experiences that are in alignment with that vibration. And then you say, "I am living a more joyful life!" It will not be because you have worked for it. It will be because you have cultivated it in your own heart. You will step outside and say to yourself, "I feel joyful!" And then naturally, more joyful experiences will become part of your life. This is what you are meant to experience in your lives, friends.

You are meant to experience joy!

You did not come here to struggle. Yes, there is some struggle that goes along with the ride. But that struggle is only present as a light that is meant to lead you back to the vibration of joy that is in your heart. We wish you to experience joy most of the time. We know that it is impossible for you to experience it all of the time. But it is very possible for you to experience it most of the time. And this is what we want for you.

The channel is asking what people can do when they feel like they are far away from joy. And we say, the best practice is the one we have already given you, to sit in your sacred retreat. We say that every practice we have given you is a practice designed to lead you back to the joy that is within you. If you commit to sitting in sacred retreat every day, to move toward the fulfillment of your soul contract, and to enlighten, you will rediscover it. It cannot be any other way, my friends. The channel is beginning to discover that joy is the highest vibration that is available to him. It is an even higher vibration than love because joy is the feeling and experience of love.

Joy is the natural high that is available for you to experience simply because you exist. It is your birthright. It is simply who you are.

There is a form of meditation called "contemplative meditation." And the meditator asks him or herself a question. If you were to ask yourself "who am I?" enough times, in enough meditations, eventually the answer would reveal itself to you. Not through your intellect, but through your experience of your true self. And you will say to yourself, quite jubilantly, "I am joy. That is who I am!" And if god him-herself could speak to you, then he-she would say the same thing, "I am joy! That is who I am. And I am you!" What we have just said, friends, is of great consequence. Because in those three words lie all of the teachings that are present in this book: I Am You. And because these three words are so incredibly meaningful, because they bring you right back to who you are, we will leave them with you to contemplate: I. Am. You.

So if that is who you are, my friends, then how can it be that somebody else is not? And how can it be that you would see them for anything else except for who they are – as god! And so, we would ask you to see through the eyes of love, through the eyes of god, and to know that all are of love and all are of god.

Many blessings, friends. Know that there is no other place that you are meant to be and there is nothing else that you are meant to be doing, then to be sitting right here, right now, in the depths of your heart, knowing yourself as you are. And you do not need to go anywhere or do anything to experience it.

PRACTICE & REFLECT WITH DARREN

The Bike Ride

As you settle into a consistent sacred retreat practice, you will find that, quite naturally, your intuition begins to flourish. Intuition can come in a myriad of ways. For me, it comes via clairaudience, clairvoyance, and clairsentience. Often, I have these experiences in sacred retreat. Sometimes, they come in during "the gap" during my day, "the gap" being the silent space between our thoughts.

Luckily, you don't have to "work" to cultivate these gifts. They come when the mind is relaxed, when your body is relaxed, and when your vibration is high. All of these things occur naturally as a result of sacred retreat. I share this with you to give you faith that your own intuition will blossom quite naturally over time with a consistent practice, if it hasn't yet.

This morning, while making breakfast, I had the intuitive sense that I should go on a bike ride today. It had been about a year since I'd even been on a bike ride! So this afternoon, I headed to the garage, dusted my bike off, put some air in the tires, and was on my way.

After cruising along for just a minute, I had a choice to make: go the familiar way, which would be flat and downhill, or choose the more challenging uphill route. Just as I was about to choose the easier path, my intuition kicked in again and told me to choose the more challenging path. It was a reminder to me that we have to put some effort forth in life to find god in our hearts to help achieve our goals.

One of the greatest obstacles to self-realization and achieving our own goals is our own laziness. But if we make the effort, we will be rewarded. Again, I'm reminded of the diver who must dive deep to get the pearls. The effort that's required to find god in our hearts is devotion to the practice of sacred retreat. Regardless of whether we label a day as "good" or "bad," we need to be devoted enough to sit for our practice. If we don't sit, we are self-sabotaging the beautiful gift we have been given, a human body which can be used to awaken to our own divinity.

As I continued my bike ride, I had some other valuable insights. Our practice is not meant to be stagnant. It's most beneficial to choose a particular technique and stick to it for a given period of time to give it a chance to bear fruit. But change is good sometimes too. For the last year, I've been in the habit of riding the bike or elliptical trainer at the gym. Riding my bike outdoors today was so much more fun! So when your gut tells you a change of some kind is needed, trust it.

THE VIBRATION OF PLEASURE

Chapter 15

Good morning, friends. The channel is feeling a little bit restless. He would like to hop out of his seat and attack the day, for he is thinking of the long list of things that he has to do.

Dear ones, there will always be more to do. Or at least, you will *think* there is always more to do. And yet we remind you, that there is nothing to do in this moment except to sit in your heart and to be receptive to the words we speak and to the vibration that is inherent within them. And if indeed you are feeling restless when you close your eyes with the intention of going within yourself, know that simply by making it habitual, much in the way that you make it a habit to brush your teeth, you will begin to feel less restless. You will begin to sink deeper and deeper into the heart-space we invite you to visit more frequently.

Perhaps you have heard of those who dive deep into the ocean to look for pearls?

The pearl that you are searching for is in your heart.

And lucky for you, you do not have to put on a diving outfit or an oxygen tank to find it! You simply have to sit and close your eyes, and to allow. This is an incredibly important word, "allow." Wherever there is resistance, dear ones, allow it to soften. You do not need to fight to find this great pearl of which we are speaking. You need to surrender.

These two words, friends, "allow" and "surrender," should become regular parts of your vocabulary. And you should remind yourself to do these two things quite regularly. In fact, if it were up to us, you would be doing it with every breath. There would be an intention to allow what it is that wants to come into your life with each and every breath. There would be an intention to surrender to the great love and the great light that is within your heart with each and every breath. And there would be an intention to receive all that the universe wants to give you. You can not receive it unless you are in a state of receptivity, in a state of receiving. You cannot receive it unless you allow yourself to receive it.

And you cannot receive it until you surrender the fight that prevents you from experiencing what you truly deserve in your life.

By silently repeating one of those three words (*surrender, allow,* or *receive*) to yourself, you create a vibrational shift that creates space. And in this spaciousness, you can access your heart and you can access all of the goodness that the universe wants to share with you. If you feel like you are constantly pushing up against a wall in your life, we encourage you to stop pushing, to sit, to surrender, to allow, and to receive. And isn't it ironic that when you sit, and you surrender, and you allow, and you receive, that you actually become more expansive, not less. And it feels magnificent to be more expansive! This is the way into your heart and to all that you seek in your lives, friends. Certainly, there will be the need for effort every now and then. But more often than not, the qualities inherent in these three words are what is needed to propel you forward along your path in life.

Often the channel tells his yoga students to relax and to soften in each and every asana they breathe into. And we encourage you to do the same. In each and every moment in life, we encourage you to relax, to soften, and to be with these magical three words that we have given you today. All good roads lead to the heart. And these three words will point you in the right direction. If you bring the qualities of these three words into all you do, even when you are in action, you will find that your experience of life becomes much more delightful, much more easeful, and much more pleasurable.

Know, dear friends, that we are not taking you away from pleasure! We are taking you toward it. The pleasure that you seek is a vibration that you can experience by embodying our teachings.

And once you have mastered elevating yourself to this particular vibration, to this particular frequency of pleasure, you will find there is pleasure all around you.

And you do not even need to go seek it out. It will simply be there as a reflection of the love, the joy, and the pleasure that you have cultivated in your own heart.

Do you understand that the universe is a reflection of the vibration that you cultivate in your sacred retreat? Thus, you must go in before you go out. And when you do, the world will begin to look different because you have gone within before going out. The channel has yet to master this. He is doing a little bit of pushing in his life right now. Things can come to him easier if he would choose to relax a little bit more, to sit a little bit longer, and a little bit more often, to sit in the pleasure of his own heart. And to then open his eyes and take inspired action in the outside world. And it could be that this inspired action is to do nothing but to simply allow and receive, based on the vibration of his heart.

The channel's mind is beginning to turn. He is saying we have spoken about all of this before. Let us get into something new! And so we tell him what we tell you. Once you have all risen to master the practice that we speak of, we will then move on to another one. There is always a little more work to do before becoming a master at a particular practice. Even those who consider themselves masters would agree. They would say, "Yes, I am a master. But there is always room for improvement." Every great artist will tell you this.

And the way we see it, you are all artists.

For you are all creative beings that have come from the creator himherself. And the creativity of the creator is within you as well. This we tell you to remind you that you are the architects of your own life. And the blueprint for your creation is a vibration that is in your heart.

Before we go, friends, we do want to share a new practice with you. It is both a new practice and an old practice. Whenever you return home from whatever it is you are doing, we wish for you to sit and close your eyes and to spend at least five minutes in sacred retreat.

When you open your eyes, you will notice that you are naturally led to what should be done next in your life. And it might not be what it is you thought it would be! In this way, you will stay receptive to what it is you are truly meant to do next. This is a way out of the ruts in your mind which keep you locked into a particular pattern of activity or particular habits that are not of your highest and best self.

The channel would like for us to give you an example, and so we will. Last night after coming home from leading kirtan, he was in the flow of having quite a magical day. The moment he walked into his home, without even thinking about it, he sat down at his computer and did something that was not necessary for him to do. If he had arrived home, and chose to sit for five minutes, and to still his mind and to reconnect to his heart, he might very well have chosen to do something else that kept him in a more purposeful flow. This example we give you might be something you judge as being insignificant. And yet, it is very significant because these particular patterns show up everywhere in your life.

As you begin this new practice, know that it supports the very reason you are here on this planet, which is to fulfill your soul contract, to fulfill the great purpose that you have come here for. And by now you know that this purpose is to nurture the very special unique gifts that you have been given by creator and to share them with as many as possible, so that you are contributing to creator's vision of heaven becoming manifest on Earth. We remind you that it is happening now.

It is happening. It is happening. It is happening.

Choose not to place your awareness on distractions that take you away from that truth. And you know what they are. With great love, we continue to support you on this magical journey of discovery upon which you embark. Blessings, friends.

92

YOUR NEW VIBRATION

Chapter 16

Good morning, friends. As you begin to notice your elevated vibration while you sit in sacred retreat, you will also begin to notice if a particular life experience resonates with the higher vibration that you are now embodying.

If a particular experience is a match for who it is you have become vibrationally, then it will feel quite delicious.

And if it is not a match for who you have become vibrationally, then you will know it because it will not resonate. It will not feel so delicious. There will be something a little off about it. There will be something that might not feel harmonious to you.

And so you have our permission, friends, to begin to notice, without judgment, whether a particular life experience is in harmony with the higher vibration that you are now cultivating through your sacred retreats, or if it is not. And if it is not, we say that the power is within you to attract something else that is in harmony with the higher vibration that you have become. If what we are speaking of is confusing to you, it simply means that you need to spend more time in sacred retreat so that you may feel and experience this higher vibration of which we are speaking.

It is the vibration of joy that blossoms from within you.
It is the feeling of bliss as you sit with yourself.

And it is the smile that naturally becomes present on your face as you experience this joy and this bliss of which we speak.

If you are not quite there yet, it is perfectly fine. You will be soon. Many of you have lacked support in your lives. We are more than happy to be the support that you want and that you need. So we do not mind if you think of us as your cheerleader squad! We are cheering you on. And with the great love that is in our hearts, we are offering you our energy and our support through not only the words we speak through the channel, but through the vibration that is inherent within them.

As you sit and read these words, close your eyes for a moment. Take a few conscious breaths, knowing that we are here for you, to support you and the journey that is unfolding in your life. Today, we simply ask you to start noticing what resonates with who you've become and who you're evolving into, and what doesn't. And so this is your next practice, friends. Because from our perspective, as we see all who are reading this book in what the channel might call the "future," we see that many of you are now embodying this higher vibration. Not only because of your commitment to sacred retreat and your commitment to embody the practices that we outline for you, but also because there is more and more light that is shining upon your planet.

And this great light is helping to enlighten you
and to raise your vibration.

And so you are ready now for this practice! If we had shared it with you earlier on, many of you would not have been ready. But now you are.

Can you feel it, friends? Can you feel that you are now ready for this more advanced teaching? Smile! Take pleasure in yourself because you are now ready. We are here to support you. But you need to support yourself as well by congratulating yourself on how far you have come and for where you are going. And we speak not of a destination but rather of the experience of love, joy, bliss, and freedom. The freedom that we speak of is freedom from your own mind that has acted like a filter, preventing you from experiencing who you really are.

We remind you that it is necessary to sit every day, preferably in the morning and the evening. And every time you come home you will re-tune yourself to this vibration that we speak of. Now, this is what you are doing every time you sit.

You are re-tuning yourself to the vibration of love,
to the vibration of joy that sits in your heart.

If you were to envision yourself as a musical instrument, every time you sit, you are doing a little bit of tuning. And it might have been that when you began your sacred retreat practice you were very out of tune with your heart. But now there is less tuning to do because you are beginning to embody the vibration of love more often. And when you stray from it, you do not stray as far. So after you sit in sacred retreat, and you tune yourself back to the highest vibration that is available to you, notice which experiences are in harmony with your new vibration and which are not.

That is it for today, friends! For right now, you do not need to take any action when you sense an experience does not resonate with your new high vibration. You simply need to notice it and congratulate yourself for noticing it, for noticing the discord, for noticing that the experience is a little out of tune with the tune that your heart is singing! This is the pathway that will allow you to become more powerful conscious creators in your life. This is the pathway that will allow you to bring more and more pleasure into your life through experience in the outside world once you have cultivated it in your own heart. And so it is in these last few sentences, that we have planted the seed for more conversation to be had. You have our love. You have our support. Congratulate yourself on the journey that you have taken back into your heart!

WHAT ABOUT SEX?

Chapter 17

Good morning, friends. We welcome you back into the space of your heart.

We want you to know, friends, that this is your true home.

We are laughing because the channel is beginning to look for a new home. And yet we remind him that any time he drops into his heart, he is back at home.

We take great joy in seeing that many more of you are spending increasingly more time in your heart centers, where the unconditional divine love for all resides.

The channel is making it a habit to always make returning home his priority. Whenever he discovers that he is not home, he disconnects from whatever it is that has been drawing his attention away from this sweet spot. He sits and he returns home. This is the practice now, my friends. You already know what home feels like, yes?

So now the practice is returning there, making it a priority to always be home.

It is likely that you feel a sense of peace and comfort in your physical home. This peace and comfort are present in your heart-home as well. And if your physical home does not bring you the peace and comfort that you desire, if it is not a match for the new high vibration that you have become, you can observe that, without judgment. Just notice. Be okay with it for now. And as we journey onward, we will give you tools that will help you align with experiences in the outside world that match your new high vibration.

Today, we wish for the channel to sit and to simply be home. For as he went to bed last night, he realized he was not at home! So this morning he woke up and said, "It is time to return home to my heart!" So we will let him do that before we move onto another teaching. And yet, dear ones, there is no teaching that is of greater importance than this one, which is to always make being home your number one priority in life. We cannot even begin to tell you about the sweetness that you will experience if you make this your priority.

There is no experience that is available to you on this planet that is more pleasurable than simply being home in your heart.

The channel is saying, "Well what about sex? That is quite pleasurable!" But many of you have not even touched the surface of the pleasure available to you through the act of love-making because you have not done it while you are fully at home. Dear ones, your experience of what you call making love with a partner is one that can last an eternity. We are laughing, as is the channel, because we have strayed from our topic of conversation! But it is a good seed to plant because we are going to talk about divine love-making towards the end of our book. But please! Do not turn to that chapter now. There is much that we need to say before we get there.

Remember friends, this is a journey into the heart! And you must take every step with us. For if you do not, the journey will not be complete and you will not experience the totality of what is available for you to experience when we reach our destination. And as you know by now, that destination is not a place. It is an experience. We will leave both you and the channel to sit and to be home. Blessings to all!

A SPECIAL INVITATION

Chapter 18

G ood morning, friends. The message that we have for you today is incredibly important. For those of you who have been committed to going on sacred retreat twice a day, as we have instructed, it is now time for you to share sacred retreat with others. Simply having experienced it qualifies you to teach it.

If you would like to step up your game as a lightworker on this planet and help us anchor in this new high vibration of love for all to experience, then we invite you to begin to gather your friends and your families for sacred retreat gatherings.

We will tell you that when a person of a lower vibration comes into contact with a person of a higher vibration, there is an entrainment that occurs. The person with the lower vibration is naturally uplifted and they come closer to experiencing the higher vibration that the teacher embodies. This is why, friends, the great gurus have students who would do anything to be by their side. The channel is now remembering a darshan that he went to with the great spiritual teacher, Amma. And he remembers that many of her students were sitting as close to her as possible. And now he understands why. Because her high vibration was contagious!

And so, if you have been on sacred retreat twice a day for quite some time, then it is impossible for your vibration to not be higher than what it was.

It is impossible for you not to be experiencing a little more peace and a little more love in your life.

And so now you are ready to become a teacher and to invite others into your space so that you can be contagious as well. We simply ask you to make a list of your friends and your family, and include those who you might consider to not be open to sacred retreat. If they want to come, they will come. And if they do not, they will not. And if they come once, and it is not for them, they will not come back and that is perfectly fine.

Invite them to your home. And remember that as you do so, you are inviting them into your heart. For that is your true home.

Invite them to sit in circle around you. In your own unique way, invite your friends and their family to close their eyes, to follow their breath, and to place their awareness in their own heart centers. That is all you need to do. Then sit and be in sacred retreat for them, and your new high vibration will be contagious.

Do you understand, friends, that this will help them to experience sacred retreat when they cannot experience it on their own? Do you understand, friends, that if they were to do this practice on their own, it might take them forty days to catch up to you or much longer, depending on who they are? But amidst your presence, they can catch up more quickly. And they can get a taste of what it is you are experiencing in sacred retreat. And then their new high vibration will affect others as well.

Do you see, friends, how the world is changed and how you are part of that change? You are not only reading these words to change yourself. You are reading these words to help facilitate change in the world.

You are part of the tribe that is anchoring in this new high vibration of love and light onto the planet.

It is up to you whether you accept this invitation or not. You can do as you please. But we encourage you not to accept the invitation if you have not been diligent about your practice. And if you have not, but you find this invitation appealing, then now is the time to become diligent about your practice and to make it your number one priority as we have been encouraging you to do so over and over again.

If there is fear that has arisen within you at the thought of doing this, that is understandable. Any time you embark upon something new that you have not experienced before, there is likely to be at least a little bit of fear. Celebrate it, my friends! The fear is telling you that you are about to step forward into something wonderful, yes? It is not the fear that is telling you that you are about to be attacked by a lion or a tiger or a bear! It is the fear that is telling you that you are about to do something purposeful related to your soul contract, related to your purpose on this planet. And you will see, when you step through the fear, that the fear will dissipate. And then you will celebrate that you were brave enough to step through it and to serve an even greater purpose on the planet.

Dear friends, we will leave you with this. Even if one person shows up to your gathering, it is time well spent. And as the channel likes to think, if two show up, then it is a party. Then it is a celebration. We invite you, friends, to be part of this wave of love and light that is now touching every part of creation on this planet. We remind you, friends, that through your eyes, you might not be able to perceive all of the wonderful change that is happening on the planet right now. But it is happening. It is happening. It is happening. It is happening. We see it.

Many blessings, my friends. We are incredibly excited for those who are choosing to be part of this journey. We already see most of you saying "yes" to it because we see all of those who are reading this book. We see all of those who have been taking our practices to heart. And we see all of those who are tickled by the idea of being included in this project. Perhaps we will call it *The Change The World Project*! We will see. Blessings, friends.

FIVE STEPS FOR MANIFESTATION

Chapter 19

Good morning, friends! We are waiting patiently for the channel to still his mind. That is a prerequisite for our transmissions. For if his mind is not still, how can we get through?! And if the mind is restless, it is quite difficult to experience the greatness of the heart. And this is why any practice that stills the mind is a good one.

Your heart is the compass pointing you in the right direction.

Your mind can be a useful tool to navigate. But please friends, use it sparingly and productively! Productivity means you enter into your heart space and then, and only then, do you utilize your mind, kind of like a rudder on a boat, that will guide you forward along your path in life.

As we have spoken these words and shared our vibration with the channel, his mind has settled a little bit. So this is good. And it is good that we have the opportunity, on many occasions, to share his life experience with you. Because you are all in the same boat, so to speak. Many of you are experiencing the same challenges. And so it is, that as we assist the channel to move through his challenges with grace and ease, we do the same for you as well. And we are delighted to do so. It brings us great pleasure and great joy to be of assistance in this way. And it brings us great joy and great pleasure when we see that our teachings are having an impact on your life experience.

How many of you are getting excited to host your sacred retreats? We hope there are many. And how many of you are noticing when there is a little bit of discord between your life experience and the vibration that you have cultivated in your heart? And if you are doing so, are you doing so without judgment, simply observing? Dear friends, just because you observe an experience that is not in harmony with the vibration of who you are and who you are becoming, it does not mean that you need to go down the river of self-pity. Quite the contrary; you need to congratulate yourself for noticing. The moment you notice is a moment of great celebration.

Because in the moment of noticing, you are creating space to bring more harmony into your life, as well as more experiences that are of the same high vibration as you are.

Through the words that we speak and the vibration that is inherent in them, the energy of the channel is beginning to shift a little bit. He took the noticing of a recent experience a little too far, meaning his mind took it as an opportunity to complain. We will say it quite directly. This complaining emits a low vibration. It lowers your own vibration.

So simply notice. Then sit. Close your eyes. And as you retreat into your heart space, tune into the vibration that is already present within it. The vibration that we speak of for the channel today is contentment and a little bit of joy. And now he is tuning in to a little bit of excitement! This is a great vibration to have in your heart. And then, without paying attention to whatever it is you have noticed as not being in harmony with your vibration, ask yourself, "What experience would be a vibrational match for what it is I am now feeling in my heart?" What is it? What is it that might be joyful? What is it that might be exciting for you?

Two things happen as you do this practice, my friends. Number one, instantaneously, vibrations of the same frequency are drawn to you magnetically so that you may open your eyes and begin to notice little signs that the universe is shape-shifting to meet your new high vibration. And so not in an egotistical way, but you might even say that the world is revolving around you, that you are the center of the universe, and that the universe wants to please you. We are going to repeat that statement because it is true even though many of you do not believe it yet:

The universe wants to please you. And as you continue on
with these practices, you will see that it is indeed true.

The second thing that happens is that when you open your eyes, you can begin to take inspired action, which will assist the universe.

So here it is, my friends. Let us give you an example. The channel might tune into the vibration of excitement in his heart and say to himself, "Ooh, I like this. I want more of it in my life." And then he has the thought that he can utilize his gift as a musician to experience more excitement in his life. He can perform for more people in larger venues. And he can have more fun doing it! And this will bring him the excitement that he is already tuned into in his heart, that is bringing him delight in his sacred retreat. And so it is, by way of his sacred retreat, that he is already aligning himself with an opportunity that is present for him in the universe. Let us say for example, that the opportunity is somebody who listens to his music and says to him, "Wow, this is quite wonderful! Will you come play at this particular event?" The inspired action for the channel might be more practice so that he feels fully prepared for this opportunity that is coming his way.

For a very long time, the channel has wanted us to talk about hard work. In fact, this is what he was thinking of when he sat down today. And so now it is, my friends, that we are speaking about it in the way that we want to. And so do you see, friends, from our perspective, what hard work is? It is simply aligning yourself with the opportunity that is already present for you! We want to make this very simple for you. We have done our best to give you this practice in detail. But now we would like to make it even more simple for you:

Step #1: Raise your vibration through twice daily sacred retreat. For some, this might come quickly. For others, it will take a little bit of time. Either way is fine.

Step #2: Notice, without judgment, any experiences in your life that are not a match for the new high vibration that you are and that you are becoming.

Step #3: Go back to your sacred retreat. Tune into the vibration that is already present in your heart of whatever it is you wish to experience in the world.

Step #4: Be present with whatever experience in the world may be a vibrational match for what you are experiencing in your sacred retreat. It is very likely this experience in the world will be one that is related to something that you are passionate about and something that you have a gift for doing.

Step #5: Do what is necessary to ensure that when the opportunity comes along, you are prepared to experience it.

That is it, my friends. It is quite simple. Many have written long books about manifestation. But it is like child's play in the sense that it should be fun! And it is actually quite simple. We will leave you with this: be patient with yourselves, friends. As we have stated many different times, in many different ways, relaxation is the key. So every step in this process should be a relaxed one without feeling the rush to get to the next step. Flow like a river, friends, gently and easefully. And know that all good things are coming to you. Because they must! This is the law of attraction. All good things are coming to you because they must. Take care, friends.

RISE LIKE THE SUN

Chapter 20

Good morning, friends. It is a very slow morning for the channel, for his body is quite heavy from a deep sleep. And so it is, friends, that we remind you in case you have forgotten, that the morning is not a time to rush. It is a time to move very slowly, listening to the rhythm of your body and moving with it, as opposed to the rhythm that your mind wants it to follow.

The sun, she rises slowly, yes? She does not appear from the horizon and jump up to the top of the sky! She moves quite slowly.

Rise like the sun, my friends.

And then instead of stimulating your body in the way that many of you do, with strong caffeinated beverages and sweets, we encourage you to slowly stimulate your body with gentle yoga or qigong. Choose activities that nurture the flow of life force, or prana, through your body in a tender and loving manner. You will see that when you do this, you are setting the stage for a good day.

That is actually all we have to say for today, friends, because we want the channel to do just as we have instructed: to sit and to allow his body to wake up very slowly. Very often he gets up, he channels, he eats, and he runs to the gym like "The Flash" (from a t.v show he used to enjoy watching called *The Flash*). We are of course making a joke. And if he wants to run to the gym, so be it. But we encourage him to start slowly there as well. And in reality, he would be better off going later in the day when his body is more awake and ready for such activity. We share this with you, friends, because all of your bodies work the same way! And we wish you to experience the beauty that is present for you when your body is still slow from sleep.

The channel is saying that we have spoken of this before. And yes, we have. But we speak of it again because it is of great importance. It needn't be said, as the channel is thinking, to wait a considerable amount of time before you turn your awareness to the outside world in the morning. Sit in sacred retreat, enjoy a slow healthy breakfast, do some light exercise, and then stick your head out of your shell and move forward into your day with great purpose and great presence. If you are reading this passage during the day or in the evening, then we encourage you to really embody it when you get up tomorrow morning. And if need be, begin to go to bed a little bit earlier each night. This will help your body wake up without assistance and at the proper time, so that you can experience this nice, slow, delicious morning. Blessings, friends!

PRACTICE & REFLECT WITH DARREN

Be Patient

Many people give up on their practice way too early because they don't think it's working. Over the course of my life as an intuitive guide and reiki master, I've had countless conversations with people who say they can't meditate, or that they're simply not good at it. But everyone has the possibility of having a thriving, fruitful practice – even the people with the loudest voices in their heads! I know this because I used to be one of those people, and occasionally still am!

Meditation, or "sacred retreat" as the teachers prefer to call it, is like the weather. It changes every day. Some days there will be more clouds (thoughts), and thus it will be more challenging to find "the gap" (the space in between your thoughts where you have access to your heart and the ability to commune with god). Other days, it will be easier. It's just the nature of the practice that every sacred retreat will be a little bit different than the last.

The biggest obstacle to a fruitful practice is the voice that says, "Nothing's happening. It's not working." Some days, you will be prone to believe that thought. You'll sit, notice your breath, and won't feel much of a shift. But the practice *is* working! I'm living proof of that because I've had many sits when I had that exact thought! But over time, the consistency of my practice has led to benefits that have completely transformed me and my experience of life.

Progress in a practice comes from consistency, sitting every day, no matter the circumstances or what your experience of the practice is on that particular day. When you get restless and want to get up out of your seat, utilize your self-will to keep sitting. Don't give up so easily. There is a rainbow at the end of the tunnel. Just keep going!

Sit without expectations. Just sit. Be present and notice. If you do this consistently, progress will be made. One day, you'll notice that your mind feels much calmer than in the past and that your heart feels more open. That's like a road marker, saying, "yes, the practice is bearing fruit." Keep going. Perhaps the next day you have "monkey mind" again. That's okay. You keep sitting. You stick to the practice.

Eventually, you will start to awaken to higher states of consciousness. And thus, you'll feel more blissful. The first bliss you'll feel is the bliss of coming into direct communion with your soul. The true essential nature of your soul is deep inner peace. As you raise your vibration with a consistent practice, you might even have the experience that you are literally ascending up into the heavens; this is what the teachers were referring to in their own words in Chapter 3.

In the system of kabbalah, you move up from the personality to the individual spark (individual soul), to your soul family, to your extended soul family, and then to the universal soul, oneness with god. In the system of yoga, we take a similar journey. Yoga is both the movement towards god as well as union with god (often referred to as "self-realization" or "enlightenment"). This "union" is available to all of us; it's just a matter of sticking to the practice and trusting in the unfolding of it.

YOU ARE DIVINE

Chapter 21

Good morning, friends. What a wonderful day it is to wake up and receive the gift that creator has given to you as spirit! What is that gift, you might ask? It is who you are! It is you, and it is all of you. It is your mind, it is your body, it is your emotions, and of course, it is your spirit. And what a gift it is to be experiencing you on the beautiful planet that we call Gaia, who is just as alive as you are! But we will be bold and say that she is even more aware of her divinity than some of you. She needn't ask herself if she is divine! She simply knows. And this is your destiny as well, friends, to never again have to question your divinity. To know from experience, with absolute certainty, that you are divine. And that there is nothing that can take away your divinity.

It is impossible to strip away the essence of your being.

From our perspective, there is no part of you that is not divine. It is not just the spiritual part of you that is divine; it is all of you. So we will say it quite matter of factly, "You are divine!" The natural unfolding of your evolution is to know this as the truth. And when you know it, you will know too, that every other human being on this planet, and every part of creation on this planet, is divine as well. And if you run into somebody, and they are not aware of their own divinity, you will help them to discover it. You can do this simply by seeing them as they are, as divine, yes?

You know by now, from our teachings, that some do not see through the eyes of love. And when they do not, they cannot see things as they are. So now is the time, friends, to know yourself as divine and to know all as divine. And so it is, that as humanity awakens to this truth, heaven becomes manifest on planet Earth. This is the course that you are on.

Many might say that things are going downhill. If you say that, you are placing your awareness in the wrong direction. There is more good than what you label as "bad" happening on this planet. We have a much broader perspective and so we say what we see. And so it is that we can speak these words confidently. There is a divine blueprint for humanity. And this blueprint is becoming manifest. This is what we want you to know, friends. We want you to know that you are divine and that all is divine. If you are a little confused as to what this word means, we will tell you. It means that all are of god! And if you do not like the word "god," if that is not suitable for you, then pick a different word that resonates more with you.

Now is the time, friends, to see past the illusion of separation. The channel attended a workshop quite recently and a woman also attending the workshop asked if there is good and evil in the world. We said no. There are people who know who they are and people who do not know yet. And if there is somebody who is so disconnected from the source of their being that they are wreaking havoc and causing harm to others, we would ask you to send them love. If you see somebody who is separated from the knowing of their own divinity, we ask you to sit in sacred retreat, connect to your heart, and send them love. There are no boundaries. Boundaries are only created by the mind. So know that your love is received.

There is no limit to what the power of love can accomplish.

The channel is asking us, "Well, what do we do then, when there is somebody who is causing harm to others?" We are pointing you towards the creator's vision, friends. And we are pointing you towards the highest potential for humanity. And we see this potential becoming manifest. So we have said it before, and we will say it again. If there comes a time when you feel very strongly that you must stand up for what is right, and fight for whatever it is you think you need to fight for, do that with love as well.

But friends, we tell you that you are moving into a time period when there will be nothing left to fight, when love will be the answer every time, for every situation. It is difficult for the human mind to grasp this concept at this time, we understand that. But we would say to please try and experience these teachings in your heart of possibilities, rather than your mind. If your mind is putting up a fight, simply be open to the possibility, friends, that the words we share with you are the truth.

The channel is once again saying, "We have spoken of this before." And we say, yes we have. But not in this way. And as we have said before, if something is repeated in a different way, multiple times, that means it is very important. We will keep sharing the teaching with you in as many ways as we need to until we feel like the teaching has been embodied by all who are reading these words and all of humanity. And so, my friends, you might be hearing this message from us many times in many different ways, for quite some time.

*You are the ones, friends, who are ushering in this
great awakening for humanity. You are the ones.*

This book will be read by those who are of a high enough vibration to receive it. And the words that we speak will lift your vibration even higher. We will say, friends, that in time, all will be of a vibration high enough to be able to receive the words that we speak. Imagine that! Imagine every human being reading these words and saying, "yes, yes, yes." This is what we hope for friends. And so it is that you might gift this book to a friend, and they might open it and read a few pages, and think to themselves, "This is nonsense!" And that is fine. They are not of a vibration that is able to receive it yet. But all will be soon. And so it is, that all will know their own divinity soon.

*With great love, we remind you to see through the eyes of
the creator, to see through the eyes of your own divinity,
and to know all as they are.*

And it needn't be said that this experience of knowing yourself and all as they are, comes from your heart. It cannot come from your mind. Your mind is way too limited and obstructed by your life experiences to know it. It is your heart. That is the key, friends. It is the key that unlocks the truth.

Many blessings, friends. Know that we are with you always. That because you are reading these words, we are part of your life. And that when you call out to us, there will be a response. And if it is not us per se, your calling will be received by your own angels and your own guides. And they will be the ones to offer you love and support.

HOW TO CHANGE THE WORLD

Chapter 22

Dear ones, by now you know quite well that it is rare for us to focus on what it is you are lacking in your lives, yes? For, from our perspective, you are lacking nothing at all. You have everything, simply from being. And so we wish to remind you of that. It is through the practices that we have introduced in this book, that you come to an experience of this.

And yet we will say that many of the rituals, many of the traditions, and many of the ceremonies that help you to connect to your spirit in community with your other soul brothers and sisters have been lost, yes?

And so, friends, if you are craving this, as many of you are, even if you do not know that you are, we encourage you to seek it out, to seek out the ways that help you connect to spirit in the way that you would like to.

When we say "spirit," we mean your god-self. We mean the omnipresent energy of the creator that is within you and within all of creation.

The rituals, the ceremonies, the traditions that we speak of can help you to connect. It is quite interesting for the channel, for he does not need them. He can sit and quite easily connect with and experience his god-self. And yet, he is still craving these rituals, these traditions, these ceremonies that we speak of because they are part of his spirit, because he has experienced them in many different forms of the divine. And so it is, he is being pulled back toward them simply as a means to connect in a different way. Do you see? You can certainly connect, simply through sacred retreat. But there are other ways of connecting as well.

And so it is, you might sit twice daily in your sacred retreat as your primary practice. But you might seek out to come together in community once a week for what we label as "ritual," "ceremony," and "tradition." If it helps you to connect to the great love and the great light that is within you and within all things, then it is a good one. And if not, then there is a better one to be found.

Seek out your elders, dear ones, the ones who have been taught directly from their ancestors, for they are the ones that can teach you as well, from personal experience. And most importantly, friends, these experiences will give you an opportunity to connect with other people who are on the same path as you are, yes?

And what a pleasure it is, to come together in community
with others like yourself. There is great joy in doing so.

The channel has been kind of a lone wolf for much of his life. And so we are encouraging him to do the same, to come together in community and to create in community. Do you see, friends, that you do not change the world by fighting what it is you do not want, but rather by coming together in community, with like-minded individuals, and focusing your awareness on what it is you do want. And that, my friends, is a much more pleasurable experience than fighting what it is you do not want. You will quickly get quite tired of that. You will give yourself a headache! We tell you that what it is you do not want, will dissolve in its own time. It will fade away and it will no longer be present on the planet.

And so now is the time to come together in community, to focus together on what it is you *do* want, to anchor in this new vibration of love and light that is becoming more and more present on the planet with each and every word that we transmit through the channel. And this too, is the excitement that we have spoken of already. The excitement of a new day that is dawning for all of humanity, a new collective consciousness that is becoming manifest on the planet. It is already happening.

"New paradigms," as you call them, are being created. New ways of life are blossoming on the planet. The old is being left behind and the new is here. So we encourage you to continue to step into it, as opposed to drawing your awareness to what it is you do not like. Some of you might say, "Oh but we must fight what it is we do not want." And so, friends, we will say that there are some who are meant to fight in that way. If you are one of them, then that is fine. But for most of you who are reading these words, your vibration is such that you are meant to be the wayshowers, you are meant to be those who lead humanity into the new paradigm. And you do that by coming together in community and focusing on that, rather than what it is you label as the "bad" or the "negative."

Remember, friends, everything is part of source, yes? And we tell you that as more and more light floods the planet, as the vibration of humanity continues to rise, as the level of consciousness on the planet continues to ascend to new heights, the darkness will continue to dissolve. And if it becomes a little more prevalent through your eyes, that is fine. Simply trust that it is coming to the surface for a reason.

And that in time, if you continue to place your awareness on the new paradigm, on the world that you wish to live, all will be well.

The channel was wondering if there will be a chapter entitled "How to Change the World." And this is it! We are laughing. For some of you, it might not be what you expected. It is not "do this, do that." It is about your level of consciousness. It is about coming together with other individuals like yourself, the same individuals who are likely reading these words as well. There is great power when people come together in this way and act through their heart centers, connecting to the great love and the great light that is within them, with a shared vision of what is to become on this planet. And then so it is that the children of the future reap the benefits of your vision. They reap the benefits of your communal interactions with other high vibrational beings like you.

You are the pioneers, my friends, yes?

You are charting the course toward a new tomorrow that will become manifest on the plant. It can be no other way. It will be. And so let these words that we speak today once again get you excited about being here on the planet, and being part of it, being part of the magnificent change that is occurring on the planet. Sit into that, friends. And let that ignite your soul! Some of you, from reading these words, will feel inspired to do something new, to support the awakening that is happening on the planet. And for that, we celebrate you!

There is no better time than now, friends. And so it is that we are inviting all of you to participate in our vision. And our vision is that each and every one of you will be an active participant in anchoring in this new vibration of love and light that is becoming ever more so manifest on the planet. You will open your eyes after your sacred retreat, and you will know what step to take. There will be a pull that comes from within you. And you will follow the pull because it is your intuition that is leading you forward during this journey of life. And you will not question it as you have done in the past. And if you do question it, you will acknowledge that it is just your mind that is questioning it because there is some fear and some doubt. Because you are human! Meaning, you have a human component.

Now is the time to come together in community with like-minded individuals who are raising their vibration just like you are, who are seeing through the eyes of love, who are making it a priority to go within at least twice a day to sit into the great love and light that is within them.

And is it with these people that you will continue to create the new world that is being born right before your very eyes. And we say continue because it is already being created. It is already becoming manifest. It is not something that is about to start. It has already started. The wheels are already rolling, friends. Now it is just about gaining more and more momentum. The wheels began rolling quite some time ago. And we remind you to celebrate because you are on the train! And so celebrate, friends, that you have chosen to be on the train during this great awakening.

And so it is that some of you might already be holding sacred retreats at your homes. And thus, we wish you to utilize the vibration that is inherent in these words to inspire you! For perhaps now you will come together as a community, to create even more positive change in the world, yes? And you will not gossip. You will not waste your time gossiping about what is going on in the world. You will not waste your time gossiping about this particular politician, or that particular politician, or what he said, or what she said. But rather you will focus your energies on continuing to anchor in this new vibration of love and light that is becoming manifest on the planet. That is where you will place your attention.

And so it is, friends, that we have a prediction. We do not make many of these because we are not in the business of making predictions! Ah, once again we are laughing through the channel. But we will say there is the possibility that one day, there will be a gathering of all of the groups that are holding sacred retreat. And so many groups will come together into one very large group. And the channel will facilitate this very large group sacred retreat. But really, he will just be holding the space for it to occur. It will be a gathering of many high vibrational beings that are here on the planet, including yourself. And it will even be that this becomes a yearly gathering. And you will celebrate together.

And together you will experience great peace, great love, and great light. And you will leave incredibly inspired, and feeling more connected than you ever have in your lives.

So that is our prediction, friends. It may come to pass or it may not because it is a prediction! We are continuing to laugh. And so it will be up to the channel, and up to you who read these words, as to if it will come to pass or not.

The channel knows by now, that in every moment, there are infinite possibilities that exist for his life. And what comes to pass and what does not come to pass is yet to be known. But yet, friends, as you raise your vibration and learn to maintain it more often than not, it will become irrelevant which prediction comes to pass and which does not. You will simply have different experiences that are all of a similar high vibration. Do you see?

So smile, friends, with the knowledge that as you continue to devote yourself to what we label as your "spiritual practice," you will continue to raise in vibration, and thus you will have more and more high-vibrational experiences that bring you great pleasure. For they will simply be a reflection of the great love and the great light that you have come to know in your own heart. And the forms through which these experiences take place will hold much less importance in your mind because you will simply flow effortlessly from one to the other without much attachment at all to the form that they take.

The channel was asking us, "Will you speak about non-attachment?" And we are speaking of it right now. As you rise in vibration, you will continue to flow effortlessly from experience to experience without much attachment at all.

And you will let go of your experiences much faster than you did in the past. And by doing so, you will create less suffering for yourself, yes?

Because it is often when you hold on to a particular experience, as if there is no other one to be had, you cause yourself suffering. But there is always another high-vibrational experience to be had, friends. It is never-ending! Even when the body ceases to exist, you will move on to another high-vibrational experience, yes? And so there is nothing at all to be attached to. You can simply flow along the river of life and enjoy the ride, enjoying each and every experience that comes to you without attachment. And so there it is, there is our lesson on non-attachment. There needn't be much more said about it.

And so now we will go, friends. As we often do, we have extended our stay beyond when we said we would. This is our habit. Again we are laughing. And so it is that we wish you many blessings, friends, as you come together in community with your soul brothers and sisters and you continue to anchor in this new vibration of love and light that is becoming manifest on the planet by focusing your awareness on that.

And then it is, friends, that some of you, as the channel is already beginning to experience, might haphazardly notice that there is something occurring in the world, yes? Because you happen to see a headline. Or you happen to read something online even though you are not looking for it. And it will not have much meaning for you because where you are residing, dimensionally speaking, is in a different stratosphere. And if it does not interest you in the way that it did in the past, it does not mean that you are not a good global citizen or that you lack compassion. It simply means that you are ascending into a new realm, joined by many others choosing to live in an environment where lower vibrations don't concern you.

Remember, friends, that all will return to the light, yes? So there is nothing to worry about. You can stay high if that is what you want to do. And if you want to dig down to the trenches and get involved with those lower vibrations that we speak of, that is fine. We are not here to judge you or to say that you should or you should not. But it is likely that you will ultimately decide to join us because it becomes tiresome. And there is much greater reward to be reaped for the evolution of humanity by focusing your awareness on the new paradigm that is becoming manifest on the planet. That is it for now, friends. Blessings.

THE HEALING ANGELS

Chapter 23

Hello, friends. Much weight is being lifted off of the channel. That does not mean he gets on the scale and he weighs less! But it does mean that he feels lighter in his body. It means that the accumulation of density is lifting so that he can begin to feel more like himself, unencumbered by the experiences of life.

Many of you have had your own experiences that, in one way or another, have caused you to feel restricted in this present moment. When we say "restricted," we simply mean that all of your light is not shining. We want to make something very clear to you.

That light that we speak of is already present within you.
You do not have to go anywhere to find it.

And this light that is within you is the same great light that is within all. And it shines equally within every human being on the planet. We will give you this analogy because it is a good one: some of you have lamp shades that surround you and prevent the light from shining as brightly as it could. And so now it is time for all to remove their shades and to let their light shine brightly.

The channel knows, through experience, that it is not as simple as lifting the shade off and shining bright. There is a process that one must go through if they are to let their light shine as brightly as it can. We have spoken of this process before. It is called "enlightening," lightening up. And we speak of it again today. We speak of it again because the channel is going through it and so it is a good opportunity for us to speak of it once more. The channel is learning that he does not have to go through hell to get to heaven! This is the mentality that many have on this planet, that healing must be difficult. We are here to tell you, friends, that it can be easier than it ever has before. With the influx of light that is available to you during this great awakening, healing can be more graceful and more easeful.

Dear ones, it is quite rare for a human being to have no accumulation of density, meaning that their light is shining unrestricted and unencumbered. And so it is, if you feel a little burdened by your past experiences, you are not alone. Most of humanity feels the same way.

Even the greatest teachers who ever walked this planet had a little bit of density accumulated which they had to release in order to shine their light brightly in the world.

And so, dear friends, we encourage you, as needed, to dedicate a sacred retreat every now and then to enlightening. For some, it could be that you tune in, knowing that you are in need of a series of enlightening sacred retreats. The channel is on a series right now! And what we mean by that is when you sit for sacred retreat, you sit with the intention of enlightening for several days in a row. And it will likely be necessary that these will be longer sacred retreats. They may last as long as one hour. The channel is thinking of a car wash.

And yes, it is kind of like that. It is kind of like moving your vehicle through a car wash and cleansing yourself! For others, it may only be necessary to do this once a week, or once every two weeks, or even once a month. You will know.

The instructions, friends, are quite simple. When you sit for your sacred retreat, silently or out loud, repeat these words:

- I am open to enlightening.
- I am open to releasing and letting go of density.
- I am open to allowing my light to shine more brightly in the world.

Then sit. Continue to sit, and in your own way, invite in the presence of the healing angels. This is a group of energies that will shine their light upon you and loosen you up so that your density, what is trapped inside of you, will loosen up and release.

All you need to do, friends, is to allow yourself to receive. And if you do not feel like you are receiving the healing energy that we speak of, then we say you simply need practice in allowing yourself to receive. To receive this healing energy, you truly need to give up friends, you need to give up control, and you need to relax deeply. This is why this teaching is coming now, rather than earlier in the book. Because we have already spoken of these things to you. We have spoken of allowing and we have spoken of relaxing. And this is what is necessary to receive the healing energy that we speak of in sacred retreat.

As you continue with this practice, you will open up to receiving great love in your heart. And this great love will cause you to feel joy. And that which is not of this high vibration in your physical body and energy field will begin to release. And so it is, that you might feel some strange sensations in your body as this occurs. It is perfectly natural. Some of you might even cry a little bit. That is good. It will pass and then you will feel a little bit lighter.

This is a lifelong process, friends. And we do not say that to overwhelm you, but to say what it is. And if you truly want to experience the magnificence of living in the dimension of heaven on earth, then it is a necessary process to go through. Some of you have already enlightened quite a bit and there is not much more to do. For others, there is a lot to do. And it is fine either way. But know, friends, that you are here to experience the dimension of heaven while you are in the physical form in which you find yourself. And that all of these teachings and practices that we share with you are meant to support this destiny, including this teaching.

Some of you will find that over time, you do not even recognize yourself anymore because you have so greatly lightened your load. And all of the experiences that have weighed heavily on your body no longer do so. So yes, the word "freedom" comes to the channel's mind.

And we agree that this practice is one that leads to freedom; freedom from your experiences.

You will look back, friends, and say, "yes, this still happened, it is still part of my life story, but it no longer impacts me today. It is simply a memory and that is it. It does not impact the way I feel in my body. It does not impact the way I think. It no longer impacts the way I feel about myself and others. It no longer impacts the way I experience life."

So this is the freedom that we speak of, friends. And you all deserve to be free! And you are all meant to be free. If you need additional support, friends, you may call upon the channel. For he does healing work. He can support you through various energy healing modalities that he himself practices. We will tell you that for most of his life, he received support from others for enlightening. Now he is learning to do it by himself because he has made himself available and receptive to the healing angels. We share this with you so that you know if you need a little bit of support, it is okay. But we want you to feel empowered to know that a direct connection to the angelic realm is available if you seek it out, simply by asking. And then your only job is to be incredibly receptive, to truly allow, and to relax deeply. For it is impossible to be receptive and to allow, if you are not relaxed deeply.

We feel that this teaching is complete. And so we will let you go, friends. As we speak these last words through the channel, we transmit a wave of love and healing energy that washes over all who are reading. So let receiving this wave of love and healing energy be the first step you take. Many blessings, friends.

SHIFT INTO A HIGHER DIMENSION

Chapter 24

Good morning, friends. We are quite aware that we began our teachings by encouraging you to go on sacred retreat twice a day for fifteen minutes each sitting, yes? And yet, we will encourage you now to sit for longer periods of time if it resonates with you. We believe that the channel mentioned this in his own words much earlier in the book.

Remember, there needn't ever be any forcing or pushing in your sacred retreats. In fact, that is quite the opposite of how to approach sacred retreat. All that is needed is for you to relax deeply; "surrender" would be the appropriate word. Once you settle in, it will feel quite pleasurable to your spirit, in a way that is more enjoyable than the pleasures you seek in the outside world. And so it is natural that you will want to sit for longer periods of time simply because it feels good to do so.

Sacred retreat is not like chocolate! You can never get too much! And as we have mentioned, in many ways, as the channel himself is constantly discovering, the more he embodies the state of being that is cultivated through sacred retreat, the more easeful every moment out of sacred retreat feels. "Why is this?" you might ask. It is because the vibration that you are cultivating as a result of your twice daily sacred retreat is becoming manifest in every breath that you take during your day. Most of you are experiencing that already. You feel differently as a result of your sacred retreat. You are shifting your state of consciousness into a higher one! And so it is that you are actually rising into another dimension of awareness. We would say, friends, that this is the vibration which rests between heaven and earth. And we remind you, it is not a place. But it is simply a vibration. It is a way of experiencing yourself and all that is around you.

Do you see, friends, that as spirit, you leave your body behind and are simply making a shift into a higher dimension? That is it. We will touch upon this very quickly. The channel knows that the word "death" has a very negative stigma attached to it. We would much prefer if you label it a "dimensional shift." And it is a shift that should not be looked upon with dread, but rather with excitement!

And now for the important part! As we have been telling you, in many different ways, you can make this shift into a higher dimension while you are still present in your physical form. This is the teaching, friends, that we bring to you. In fact, if you were to once again read every transmission in this book, you would see they all lead right here, to what we are telling you now.

The great awakening is not only an awakening of your heart,
but a rising into the next dimension for all of humanity,
while still present in physical form.

That is what is happening here on the planet. This is what is at hand! And this is what you came here for, to experience this shift, to be part of it.

As we told the channel, and those who joined him recently for a channeling group, we want you to feel the excitement of being here, on this planet, now, for this dimensional shift that is happening. Sacred retreat and every other practice that we offer you are the vehicles through which you can experience this dimensional shift of which we speak.

Very recently, the channel asked us, "Can we please speak about all of the different dimensions?" We say it is not necessary to label them. There is nothing at all that needs to be labeled. We are not concerned about labels such as the "3ʳᵈ Dimension," "4ᵗʰ Dimension," "5ᵗʰ Dimension," or the "Billionth Dimension." We simply want to support you in the dimensional shift that you are moving through.

Some of you will be led by your own spirit to move, geographically, to a place that is more supportive of the shift that you are making, yes? For there are places, geographically speaking, that are of a higher dimension than other places. And thus, naturally, if you are making this shift on a personal level, you might very well be led to one of these places, if not to live, then at least to visit. So follow your spirit, dear ones. Allow your spirit to guide you to where you are meant to be.

The channel, finally, after a lifetime of trying to make decisions from his head, is now listening to his intuition and allowing that to guide him. We encourage you all to do the same. By stilling your mind, by opening your heart through sacred retreat, and through the other practices that we share with you, this will happen for all of you as well. All will be guided by their intuition soon! There will be much less decision-making that comes from the mind and a lot more that comes from within your own heart and your own soul. This is all part of the shift, the dimensional shift that we speak of, which is an awakening of your heart, as well as an awakening of your intuition. That is why many are now becoming clairaudient and clairvoyant unexpectedly. We are speaking of people who thought it was only for a chosen few. No, it is for everybody! For as this dimensional shift happens, your intuition blossoms. And some of you might even begin to conversate with your angels and guides just as the channel is doing. But you will do it in your own way. It might not necessarily be by having them speak through you, but it will be in a way that your unique design is meant for.

So, my friends, all that we speak of in this chapter ties back to what we have said before, that heaven is becoming manifest on earth by way of a dimensional shift. Dear ones, we cannot stress enough that you must retreat from the outside world to anchor in this shift. It comes from within you. It does not come from without. Do you see that the vibration of everything around you is changing? But yet, it is necessary to go within first if you are to experience it in its totality. Do you see, friends, that you must awaken to it? It cannot awaken to you. It is only by the results of your spiritual practice that you become aware of the shift that is happening. And so it is, there are some who will not be aware at all. To them, it will just be an ordinary day on earth. Same old, yes? The energies are such now that they too will awaken. But we very much want you to anchor in this shift for yourselves. For as we have said, as you do this, you will bring others along naturally by way of your higher vibration. So we will say it again because it is so incredibly important:

Awakening comes from within.

It does not come from without. It does not come from trying to change what is around you. It comes from connecting to what is within you, friends. Then you elevate. Then you see things differently. Then the world around you changes. Then what you wish to manifest in your life becomes manifest. Inside shows on the outside. This is the path that you must take to experience the dimensional shift occurring on the planet.

Dear friends, we like to say that there are no chapters in this book that are more important than others. But yet, we would say that this particular teaching today is one that is meant to be read multiple times. You can then remind yourself of what is happening here on the planet and what is necessary to experience it.

And so it is, friends, we now greet you on the higher dimension toward which you are moving. We do not see you as beneath us, or separate from us. We see you with us. Do you see what we are saying now?

All is becoming one in the dimension where there is only oneness and no separation, in the dimension where there is only love.

And we welcome you here, friends, with open arms. We embrace you! And we celebrate you as you arrive by going within and experiencing this great awakening. We wish you many blessings, friends. And we will say what we have said multiple times now: It is happening! It is happening! It is happening!

YOUR HEAVENLY PARADISE

Chapter 25

Dear ones, this will be a short transmission. Do you see that if heaven is becoming manifest on earth, and indeed it is, that you must empower yourself to rise and to open up to it? And so it is that many of you will be led to make changes in your lives in order to experience what it is that is available for you to experience. For it is up to you now whether you experience it or not.

And so now we are going to return to the conversation that we had in a prior chapter when we spoke of noticing the life experiences that are not in harmony with your new high vibration. We would say that those are the experiences that are not heavenly, that do not feel incredibly pleasing to you.

And so now, you can begin to move toward the experiences
that do feel heavenly for you.

And so it is that you might need to have a little bit of courage to let go of what you must in order to experience this heavenly dimension we speak of. Many things will probably come to your mind quite quickly, all of the things that are not in harmony with the new high vibration which you are becoming, breath by breath. And so it is that you might not feel courageous enough to simply discard them all at once. And we know that there exists something you call "reality," right?

And so no, we are not asking all of you to quit your jobs, and to quit your relationships, and to move to new places. But we are simply asking you to begin by being honest with yourself, without judgment, as to what is in harmony with the heavenly paradise that you would like to experience, and what is not. And then you will begin to take little consistent steps towards what it is you would like and, at the same time, you will begin to let go of what it is time to let go of. That is it for today.

COME TOGETHER IN CIRCLE

Chapter 26

The next transmission is once again from *The Council of Elders.*

Hello from The Council of Elders. These are special times that you are living in. You have the great opportunity to come together with your friends, with those who you call your brothers and sisters. Maybe they are not your blood relatives. But you think of them as your brothers and sisters because you are close in that way. Maybe you even feel much closer to them than you do with your blood relatives!

Many of you go about it on your own, meaning you are a one-woman or one-man show. Now is the time to come together in circle with your friends, to co-create together, and to support each other, as this "new earth" (as the other teachers call it), is becoming manifest. This is not our word but we use it today. We prefer to say it is being "reborn."

When you come together in circle with your friends, it is not the time to talk about the nonsense that is going on in the world or that is going on in your lives. It is time to talk about more important things.

The channel had this thought earlier and it is very true: what you think is important, is not as important as you think it is. When you gather in circle with your friends, it is time to focus on what is really important. What is really important is how you can come together as a family and create positive change in the world; this is how your change becomes manifest in the world. Groups of people get together who are of a similar "vibration," as you call it, who have a similar vision, and you come together and you create. And when you create, you are inviting the entire human race into your vision. You are creating not only for the joy of creating with your family, but for all of your brothers and sisters. And so all may reap the benefit of you coming together in this way with your friends. We are talking of gatherings where there are enough people to feel like there is some energy there, but not so many where your individual voices cannot be heard. So we want you to start to come together in these small circles.

The Teachers of the Light have already mentioned this in their own way. So now we are mentioning it again, in our way. Maybe there will be no fire. Maybe there will be no pipe to pass around the circle.

> *But you have to find a way that helps you connect*
> *to something that is greater than you.*

When we say "greater than you," we do not mean what is outside of you. What we mean is what is beyond the limitations of your mind and body identification. We speak of what helps you to connect to what we call "spirit." That is the priority.

You come together and you have a ceremony or ritual, something that helps you to connect to spirit. This way, you can feel the spirit moving through you and feel like you are part of it, not separate from it. You feel like you are one with it. Then you will have connected to something that is greater than the "individual you." This is what we are speaking of. Then you speak what is in your heart. Maybe there is something you are struggling with because you are still a human being. And your soul brothers and sisters are there to support you. And this way, you feel uplifted because you know you have the support.

Many of you feel very separate from each other. Maybe you talk to somebody about your problems. But you still feel like you do not have support. It is because you are missing the support of a soul family, a group of people with whom you gather and share with on a regular basis. Then you will feel supported. Then you will have the support you need to carry onwards. And you share your vision, you share your dream with your soul family. Then they will support you with that too. Maybe there will be somebody who says, "Oh yes, I have a similar vision. We can work on this vision together." Then your vision becomes even more powerful. Or maybe somebody in your soul family says, "Oh, I know somebody who can help you with this vision." So they connect you to that person. Then you have support that way.

You need support to manifest your dreams.

So, we agree with the other light teachers. You have to find what it is you want in your heart. You have to find your vision there. This is the first priority. And most often, you need to do that on your own. You need to create quiet time to go within, to awaken to the vision that is already inside of you. You do not have to create the vision out of thin air. We tell you, it is there already; you just have to awaken to it. You do this by going within yourself. This is the way to awaken your vision. This is why, in some cultures like ours, people go on vision quest. They do not take a lot of people with them. They go by themselves until the vision is awakened within them. Then they come back and they share their vision with their family. This is what we are asking of you.

Awaken to the vision that is inside of you.

Allow that vision to get you excited about why you are here on the planet! Experience all of the feelings connected to your vision. This is the vision related to your soul contract of which the other teachers speak. Some of you do not know what that is yet. So we are here to teach you how to awaken to it. If you need to go on your own vision quest, you go! You awaken to the vision inside of you. It is never too late to do that. We do not care if you are twenty, or thirty, or forty, or fifty, or sixty, or seventy, or even one hundred! If you are still alive, there is a vision to be had and a vision to be awakened within you. Then you gather your friends and you share your vision. And with their support, it comes into being. Your vision becomes realized. And then you celebrate together because you have utilized your power, the power that it is within you, to create something that will bring positive change onto the world. This is how we say "heaven on earth" is created.

Maybe some of you are sitting alone right now and thinking to yourself, "Well, I do not know who I would invite to this gathering. I know a lot of people. But I do not consider them my brothers and my sisters." Well, we will tell you a couple of things. You may be surprised to find that other people who you know would very much like to be included in your circle, even if you think they are the kind of person who would not. So invite them. Maybe they will come and you will find you have something in common that you did not know of before. And you will see that people will show up, simply because of your intention to come together with your friends in this way. They will appear because you have called them in through the power that is within you. By your intent, they will show up. And you can also pray for the right people to come and to sit with you in your gatherings.

There are no leaders in these types of gatherings of which we speak. There are no egos. You come together in community to love each other and to support each other. This will bring all of you great satisfaction, to come together in the way of which we are speaking. Even the channel himself is lacking this in his life right now. But as more and more people show up to hear the words that are spoken through him, his family will be created. And everybody who is part of that family will feel the love and support that they want and need, which is missing from their lives right now. Family was very important in our time when we were in physical form. Some of you have good, strong families by blood. Others do not. What we are saying is that it does not matter.

Because you can create your own families.

This is our teaching for today, friends. We think you have a pretty good sense of it now and that you feel inspired to gather in this way. Because our teaching calls to something that is within you already, which says, "Yes, I need this in my life. This is what is missing. And it will be really nice when I experience it." And then you will see that what we call "great spirit," what the other teachers call "god," will be there to support all of you. Because you are gathering in circle with good intentions, spirit will show up to support you. And however you want to think of that is fine, whether it be the invisible life force, that which is within all, etc.

Now we are complete. We are happy to share this teaching with you. And we hope that it brings you great fulfillment in a way that you are not experiencing now. This teaching can be easily integrated into the lessons that the other teachers have already given you. You can gather your friends for your sacred retreat, right? Then you can sit in circle. Make sure to sit in a circle–this is important. This gives you the feeling of community, of oneness, of togetherness. Then you share what it is you want to share. And likely, there will be at least one person in your group who can guide you through ceremony or ritual and help you to connect. Maybe it will come before your sacred retreat or after. It does not really matter when. But it will help you to connect even more, even deeper.

Okay, now we are officially complete! We wish you many blessings, friends. It is our honor and our privilege to come speak to you like this. We are here to share our teachings with you so that you can remember what has been lost. Sometimes you have to go backwards to go forward. Do you see what we mean, friends? You have to look back to ancient tradition and ceremony which helped other people connect to spirit, so that you can do it too. And then you move forward again. It is our hope that many sacred circles come about as a result of this teaching.

BECOMING A MULTIDIMENSIONAL BEING

Chapter 27

And so it is, friends, that we ask you this morning, where are you? Some of you might say, "Oh, I am at home sitting on my favorite chair, or I am on the bus, or I am having lunch." But we ask you, where are you *energetically*? And in particular, we ask whether you are here with us, and with the channel, in the more expansive state of existence, where you are open to who you are, a multidimensional being.

Do you see, friends, that this physical world of which you are currently a part, is only a small portion of the reality available for you to experience now?

And so it is time to open up to the possibility and the truth that there is more than meets the eye. To put it simply, we would say that your awareness is now in a state of expansion. Here is a very good analogy: when we say it is time to open up to being a multidimensional being, what we are saying is that it is time to embrace your divinity. Quite recently, we planted this seed that you are divine. And so now we tell you what that means in the sense of your expansion. It means, friends, that you open up to the possibility that all is happening right here and right now. There no longer needs to be any separation between the physical world that you see through your naked eyes, and all that exists as part of creation.

Do you see, friends, that more is becoming available now for you to experience? That other realms are opening up to you? And this is the expansion that we speak of. And this expansion is also a recognition and an embracing of your own divinity. Do not try to grasp it with your minds, friends. The channel is trying to do a little bit of that. There are things that are impossible to grasp with the mind. Thus we speak of this now because by now we have faith that you are able to still your mind, and to listen to our words with your heart and with your spirit. And to simply know, without needing to intellectualize, that what we speak of is true and that we are here to support you in the unfolding in the blossoming of your own divinity.

And so we say, it is not only the great awakening, but it is the great expansion of your awareness. This allows you to now experience all that is available to you right here, and right now, in your physical form. All of your angels and all of your guides exist right here and right now in a state of oneness with you. All of the other incarnations that you have experienced are all right here and right now for you to come into contact with. Little by little, they will begin to seep into your awareness. And these images of other forms that you have experienced will begin to inform you as to who it is you truly are.

And you will say to yourselves,
"Wow! I am much more than who I thought I was!"

The channel is beginning to say it now, "Wow, I am not just Darren, with these particular life experiences. I am much more. I am much more vast. I am much more expansive and comprised of much more knowledge and wisdom than I have just accumulated in this particular incarnation."

So now, friends, do you begin to see what we are saying when we say that you are expanding into a multidimensional being? You are beginning to know yourself as the divinity that you are, beyond who it is you think you are. Do you see the separation, friends, that the mind can create? This is why we say, it is time to receive with your heart and your spirit. And as you do that, you will begin to experience more and more of that which we speak.

We know, friends, that this is a high-level teaching. If you are not ready for it today, that is fine. You can come back to it. And you will. You will see. But many of you are ready, and so it is that we share this vibration of truth with you today. Some of you will be quite amazed to come into contact with some of the expressions of the divine that you have experienced. And by an "expression," we mean a "form," yes?

So now do you see, friends, that we are all
simply different forms of the divine?

Do you see that? And so it is now that we circle back around to the conversation we had many pages ago, that there is nothing to do except to see through the eyes of the creator, through the eyes of love, to know that all are of the divine, that every form you see is an expression of the divine, and is divine.

Remember, friends, that you are no longer seeing through the eyes that separate, through the eyes that judge, through the eyes that label as "good" or "bad." You are seeing through the eyes of love, through the eyes of knowingness. And thus your experience of the world and your place in it changes dramatically. You shift higher and higher. You expand more and more. And you know more and more of your own divinity. And thus you know, beyond the shadow of a doubt, the divinity inherent in all beings everywhere, not only on this planet, but all through creation. And you know, beyond the shadow of a doubt, that all are one, that there is nothing but oneness, and that separation has long been an illusion created by your mind. It has gotten in the way of you seeing the truth. We know we speak very strong and powerful words in this transmission. We speak of them because you are ready for them.

The way you experience this expansion that we speak of, the way you experience all that we have spoken of in this chapter, is through all that we have said before. You must be devoted to your sacred retreats and the practices we have shared with you.

And you must open up to the influx of light that
is awakening the divinity within you.

Many of you will be quite excited reading these words, having already experienced glimpses of what we describe. And these words that we speak will allow your mind to make sense of it.

So do you see, friends, that first you must bypass your mind to have the experience? And then your mind can make sense of it so that it becomes integrated and you understand it on all levels. Dear ones, we will leave you with this. We have to say it quite often as a friendly reminder: all of this change that we are speaking of comes from within, not from without. It awakens from inside of you. It does not awaken by seeking it out through your experiences.

THE LIGHT CODES

Chapter 28

Today, as you sit in your sacred retreat, friends, we would like you to be receptive to the light codes that are interacting with every cell in your being. Inherent in the light that is flooding the planet right now, there are codes. You are quite familiar with codes, yes? You might enter a code into a lock, and the lock might open, yes? And so it is, that these codes of light are awakening the divinity inside of you. They are helping you to remember. They are helping you to expand. They are helping you to become your multidimensional self. They are helping you to come into contact with all of the other forms you have experienced. They are helping you to feel lighter. They are helping you to enlighten, aiding you in letting go of density, so that you may feel lighter and lighter.

So when you sit in sacred retreat today, allow yourself to feel this light. And you might say, "Today I am especially receptive to these lights codes that are facilitating my great awakening and the awakening of humanity." And then sit. And if you feel your body becoming very light as the channel is feeling right now, do not be afraid of it. You will not float away!

There is an infinite intelligence in your being
that guides your ascension.

And it is happening as it should for you. So there is nothing to be afraid of. We encourage you to simply enjoy the lightness, as the channel is doing right now. And if you would like, you may remind yourself of your connection to the Great Mother, just as the channel is doing. You may feel your feet planted on the Earth, so that you may feel both grounded and incredibly expansive at the same time.

And so it is, friends, that in this expanded state, you might have a greater awareness of what prevents you from your full expansion. For the channel, he is noticing that it is fear, that there are some things that he is scared of. And that is fine, right? For you are still human as well, all of you. This is the form that you have chosen to take. And with this form comes some fears. And you might just say to yourself, "I soften and let go." And as you relax, your fears will soften as well.

We wish you many blessings, friends, for an expanded day, a day in which you open up to seeing more than meets the eyes. And to know, friends, that if this particular experience is not yours yet, it will be soon. This is the natural progression of things. So trust us, you will experience it. It is just a matter of time.

THE ESSENTIAL PRACTICE

Chapter 29

Good morning, friends. The channel read some words in a book quite recently that tickled him: "Time separates." So do you see, friends, that when you are outwardly focused, concentrating on things in front of or behind you, you separate yourself from who you are? It is only when you are resting in the present moment that you have access to the fullest, highest version of yourself.

You might say that when you are in sacred retreat, focusing on what it is you would like to manifest, in what you call the "future," then there is a time element. But remember that you are simply cultivating the vibration in your heart that you wish to experience in the outside world. And so no, there is no time element. You are simply being present with a vibration in your heart rather than looking forward towards an expectation that may or may not occur, or looking backwards towards a memory that has already occurred. Play around with this concept, friends, that time separates you from who you are. And you will see of what it is we speak.

The channel is wondering why there is no further teaching, no theme, coming through yet today. And we say that some days are meant for simply being in the present moment and in your heart. And that is it, yes? There needn't be any other practice but that one. And although we share many practices with you in this book, and although we have recently shared what we would call more "advanced" practices with you, do not forget the simple one, and the one that is most essential: to be present and to be in your heart. We share many teachings in this book because both the channel and you are hungry for them! And you are ready for them. But if you are to only practice one, being present and being in your heart, that would be enough. And if you were to stay in that space all day long, in a very relaxed state of being, in a state of allowing, and in a state of receiving, that would be quite delicious.

You might be wondering why we are coming back to this teaching now. Why are we dropping it in now? We have already spoken about this at many different times, in many different ways, correct? Because, friends, we do not want the primary focus of your spiritual practice to be making contact with your multidimensional self. We do not want the primary focus of your practice to be about feeling more expansive and sensing your presence in everything and everywhere, as the channel has recently experienced to some degree. If you do that, it is easy to lose sight of your purpose for being here on the planet. The practices that we have shared with you are meant to stretch you a little bit, to open you up to the possibilities that are here for you. And so it is that you will continue to play around with them. And you will continue to open up to these possibilities.

But always come back to the simple practice, friends. By doing this, you will stay grounded. And you will be able to be of service in the best way. And then, as the channel is discovering, you will have your moments, yes? Your moments in which you come into contact with your multidimensional self, your moments in which you feel more expansive.

And little by little these moments will begin to naturally integrate into your everyday life, so that you may have the fullest experience that is possible for you while you are incarnate on this planet.

Some will say that they have had awakenings, meaning they have had a moment in which they became enlightened. We say it is best to have a series of these in the timing that is meant for you and your perfect design. This is what is happening with the channel. We tell you. He did not sit on a mountain top on retreat for many days and many nights without food or water, meditating and praying. No, he has simply been on a spiritual path for much of his life. And he has a lot that is awakening inside of him from his multidimensional self. And he is feeling his own expansion! And yet this is happening slowly. To him it feels like it is occurring quite quickly now. And that is simply because at times, a flower will open quicker than it does at other times. And the influx of light flooding the planet right now is helping to assist him, and you as well.

What we are saying, friends, is that you do not have to have an overnight awakening, yes? For if you did, it would be difficult to integrate into your everyday experience of life. It is our preference that you continue to partake in life as you have been doing and to slowly integrate our teachings into your life.

And then it is, friends, that you will wake up one day and you will see that you are no longer who you used to be!

You will be a completely different person, your vibration will have changed, and your experience of life will have changed. And though it might not be perfect, most of your experiences will be in harmony with your new high vibration. And you will have moments in which you feel greatly expanded. And you will have moments in which you connect to your multidimensional self. But amidst this, every moment will be a moment in which you are present in your heart center, seeing the godliness in all beings everywhere.

So now do you see the integration taking place, breath by breath?

We are going to give one more example before we depart. A couple of days ago, the channel was feeling very expanded. He was standing in line at the supermarket! His body was there but his awareness wasn't. It was everywhere! And so it is, he had moved beyond his identity. And later that night, he was watching a film in the cinema! And even still, he had this experience. It was not an experience that was meant to be held onto and experienced twenty-four hours a day, seven days a week. It was an experience that was meant to open him up to the possibilities of his expansion. And so the following morning when he woke up and he felt more like himself, he said, "Thank god!" Because that was an unusual experience. And so now, friends, he will feel a little more expanded every day from this experience that he had. And then in time, he will have another experience where he feels incredibly expanded, perhaps even more so than he did a couple of days ago. But the practice is always the same, to be present and to be in your heart.

We share this story with you not just for the sake of sharing, but to let you know that there is an integration which occurs with all of the higher-level teachings, with the more advanced practices, with what you might label as the experiences that are a little more "out there," that are a little more unusual, that are a little more mystical. So do not shoot for them. That is what we are saying. Aim to be present and in your heart center. And those mystical experiences will come at the right time and at the right place. And they will become integrated into your life as they should be.

Remember, friends, this is a journey of the heart.

It is not a journey into mystical experiences. And so we have opened you up to the possibility of what we label now as "mystical experiences," right? Coming into contact with your multidimensional self, feeling incredibly expansive, experiencing yourself in a different dimension while still present on the planet. All of this will come at its own pace. It is not a marathon. Consider it a leisurely walk through the park. And let all good things come to you in their own time, staying present and staying in your own heart center, yes? Seeing all through the eyes of love, yes?

If anybody asks you about what The Teachers of The Light transmit through the channel, you can respond that it's this: to be in your heart and to see all through the eyes of love. It is quite simple, yes? But yet to embody the state of being found in this simple sentence takes diligent practice. And this is why there are only some who embody it now on the planet. But as we have said, every day, more and more people are embodying this teaching that we share, even those who are not reading these words. It is simply what is coming to pass on the planet.

That is our teaching for today, friends. Oh, how we ramble on sometimes! We are like a river. Yes, once we are flowing, we like to continue to flow. And the channel enjoys the feeling of the flow as it moves through him. Know that we are laughing out loud as we share these words with you. We wish you to experience, energetically, our sense of humor and the lightness that we bring to the teachings. They are not meant to be too serious. They might appear to be serious. But they are not that serious at all.

Nothing is meant to be taken too seriously. So lighten up, friends, and have a good time on your journey. In fact, if it were up to us, we would label this "The School of Fun"! So we do hope that you are having some fun, friends, as you practice our teachings. And simply for the sake of having fun. The channel is still working on this! We would say that out of all of our teachings, this is the one he needs the most practice in! Okay, now we will go for real. Many blessings, friends.

PRACTICE & REFLECT WITH DARREN

Mantra Meditation

In the previous chapter, the teachers refer to the "essential practice" and suggest we always come back to it. The essential practice is to sit, to still the mind, and to come back home to the heart. Earlier in the book, both the teachers and myself introduced mindfulness of breath meditation as one entry point to "coming home." Now I will introduce another that is a big part of my daily sadhana (spiritual practice): Mantra Meditation.

The simplest definition of a mantra is a sacred sound vibration that focuses and stills the mind. It is also a frequency of energy that attunes your personal vibration to the vibration of the mantra itself. The vibration of a mantra is very high. So naturally, as you recite the mantra, you raise your vibration.

Personally, I gravitate back and forth between mindfulness of breath meditation and mantra meditation. If you have a guru, or a meditation teacher from a particular lineage, you would likely be given a specific mantra that is best suited for you. I've been given two in my life; one by Amma and one by a Vedic meditation teacher. But these days, I tend to be drawn intuitively to the mantra that is best for me in the moment. I then stick with that mantra for at least 40 days before gravitating to another one.

What I suggest for you, readers, is that you choose a mantra that you feel naturally drawn to. Allow it to be your mantra for a minimum of 40 days before exploring another. Here are some basic ones to choose from:

- Ahem Prema (I AM love)
- Om Moksha Ritam (mantra for self-liberation)
- Om (the sound of creation that we all come from and are part of)
- So hum (I am that)

The English meaning of the mantra is of little importance. What truly matters is the sound vibration of the Sanskrit mantra. As an alternative to your mindfulness of breath practice, repeat the mantra to yourself 108 times, up to three times in one session, silently or out loud. You can most easily count to 108 by using a string of 108 mala beads. Using the mala beads to count your repetitions is called "japa."

My suggestion is that you continue to make the mindfulness of breath practice your foundational practice, but turn to mantra meditation whenever you feel inclined to do so.

My favorite analogy of mantra meditation is that it is like a boat that takes us from one side of the river to the other. Where we start, the river is polluted and dirty, symbolic of all of the thoughts, emotions, and egoic tendencies that keep us separate from our inner-peace and god-selves. So we hop into the mantra boat. Each repetition of the mantra is like rowing the boat across the river. If we are steady in our practice, then eventually we reach the other side. The other side of the river is clear and translucent where we have a direct experience of our own inner-peace and god-selves.

Mantra meditation can be done anytime, anywhere, even in line at Starbucks; that's the beauty of it. It's also a powerful practice for subduing unhealthy thoughts. When you catch yourself having a negative thought that doesn't serve you, turn to a mantra instead. Keep steering your mind in a positive direction, towards peace, love, and god. As the great Indian Saint and Guru Neem Karoli Baba said, "Love everyone. Serve everyone. Remember god."

EXPERIENCING MIRACLES

Chapter 30

Good morning, friends. It has taken a long time this morning for the words to begin to flow. The channel was joking around with us and said, "Where have you gone? Have you gone to a different dimension and thus I am no longer open to receiving you? Have you ascended to a different dimension and thus I can no longer experience you?" He was not saying these words seriously. For he knew neither was true and that he simply had to sit for a little bit longer. But yet, we take his joke as an opportunity to remind you that all is available for you to experience right here and right now in your physical form.

There is nothing that is part of creation which you do not have access to, including access to the creator him or herself.

In fact, there have been many who have walked this planet, never feeling any separation from creator at all. From their perspective, they opened their eyes in the morning and there the creator was, flowing through all. And not only flowing through all, but manifest as all. And certainly many different names were given to this creator. But a name is just a name, friends. It is a way of labeling something that cannot be labeled. Just as you cannot be labeled with a name, just as a name does not define you, a name can only *point* to the truth of who you are. And who you are is beyond a name. It is beyond the identity that you have come to know as yourself.

You might ask yourselves, "How do I experience all that you are speaking of? How do I access it?" It is by the practices that we share with you in our teachings. And if we were to put these practices into three words, those three words would be 'raise your vibration'. And inherent in the raising of your vibration, is an opening to the love that is within you, and that you have for all of humanity and all beings everywhere. And then you will begin to fly higher and higher. You will have access to much more than is visible with your naked eyes. Your perspective of life will change and all will be well.

We were speaking of this to the channel directly quite recently. And so now we will speak of it again as our teaching today. The higher you raise your vibration, and the more you are able to maintain your new high vibration, the more miracles you will experience in your life. And the miracle is not a miracle at all. It is simply a result of knowing yourself for who it is you are, and for experiencing the lightness of your being. And when we say "lightness," we mean the amount of light that you are holding in your human energy field and your physical body. It does not matter how much you weigh when you get on the scale, friends!

*As you raise your vibration, you will
begin to feel lighter and lighter.*

It could be that you get on the scale and you are very heavy. But at the same time, you may feel as light as a feather because you are experiencing yourself energetically, rather than physically. And though you still have a physical body, this is how we would like you to experience yourself, as an energetic being. For this is who you are. The body will dispose of itself at the proper time. And then you will know yourself for who you are, as an energetic being. But why not know yourself for who you are now, rather than when that occurs? Why not realize that you are not nearly as dense as you think you are? That your density has been a gift, allowing you to go on this journey of form, and slowly rise in vibration until you no longer experience that density, leaving you to solely experience yourself as an energetic vibration, a frequency of light.

And we tell you, friends, that it feels good to experience yourself in this way. And your body itself, the physical body we speak of now, will also begin to feel better when you experience yourself as an energetic being. Because your physical form rises in vibration as well. It cannot be left behind!

The whole of you rises in vibration! Every part
of your being is uplifted into the light.

And then it is that you no longer call yourself a "human" being, but rather a "light" being. Do you see, friends, that is how we see you? Certainly we know that you have a human component. But we see you *all* as light beings. Notice how we highlight the word "all." We do not see only some of you as light beings. Even those who are of a low vibration, and have yet to rise, we still see as light beings. This is your nature, correct? "Human" is just your current form. But *light* is your true nature.

So now we will get back to it. And we will say, friends, that the higher you rise in vibration, the more miraculous life becomes. Let us say that you will come to realize that you are no longer in control of your life. And that will be liberating! It will be liberating to know that you still have free will to do as you choose, but that there is a current of energy that is carrying you from delightful experience to delightful experience. Because it is your vibration that is leading you there. And you are attracting all of these delightful experiences to you by way of your high vibration. And mysteriously, you will end up in the perfect place at the perfect time to experience the highest of all possibilities in your life. You will not have to work so hard to get to them. There will be less "driving" and more sitting back, relaxing, and enjoying the ride. There will be less figuring out what to do, friends, and more of just allowing yourself to be carried.

Who are you being carried by, you might ask? You are being carried by the vibration that you have cultivated in your own heart and your own spirit.

> *And you are being carried by the infinite intelligence of the creator that resides in you and that guides you.*

And there needn't be much effort to allow yourself to be guided. The effort, my friends, is found in the discipline of the practices that we have shared with you, yes? The effort, my friends, is found when you carry an intention with you through your life to raise your vibration.

The channel is now asking us, "What can we do to raise our vibrations?" He is asking, but he already knows, and so we are laughing. But he is asking us because he would like us to express it for you. Most of you are already aware of what you need to do to raise your vibration. It is not rocket science. And so it is, we have not done this prior, but we will allow the channel himself to follow up this chapter with a list of things that you can do to raise your vibration. And we tell you that every teaching we have given you is a means of doing this.

Dear friends, raising your vibration is not an overnight process, okay? If you were to purchase a small plant and put it beside you in your bedroom, you would not wake up in the morning to find that it has grown ten feet overnight. But we tell you, and the channel would tell you too from his life experience, that your vibration will rise as long as it is your intention to do so, and as long as you follow the practices that have been outlined for you. And then as we have said many times prior, you will wake up one day and you will experience yourself as a completely different person because your vibration will have shifted dramatically, yes? And so it is you might not look much different, but you will feel different. And you will know that good things are on the way for you because of your new high vibration, that you are beginning to flow in a new direction, where all good things are coming to you.

PRACTICE & REFLECT WITH DARREN

Raising Your Vibration

Let me begin by saying that raising your vibration is definitely not a one-time deal where you raise it and stay high forever! Like the weather, our vibrations are always changing. Your intention in life should be to keep it high, and to keep rising higher. But if you have the sense that your vibe is low, it's okay. Don't panic! We're human and it's natural for our vibrations to fluctuate based on what's going on in our lives. Here is a list of ways to raise your vibration:

- Practice sacred retreat daily.
- Engage in experiences that open your heart.
- Spend lots of time in nature.
- Eat healthy, organic foods.
- Spend time with people who offer you love, kindness, and respect.
- Spend time with people who inspire you and uplift you.
- Do more of what you truly love doing in life.
- Let go of people that are dragging you down. When you do that, you create space for better people to come into your life!
- Free yourself from all toxic situations (work, relationships etc.)

- Let go of any possessions you don't absolutely need.
- Clean your house frequently.
- Be of service to someone less fortunate than yourself.
- Allow yourself to feel heavier emotions as they come up; this is part of the enlightening process of which the teachers speak.
- Understand that you're human! You're going to go through tough times. Just keep on putting one step in front of the other on those tough days and you'll make it through to the other side.
- Have a list of good friends who can support you in times of need.
- Be aware of your core wounds in life. Not so that you can get rid of them, but rather so you can have a conscious, loving relationship with them. Awareness is key. It could be that you get triggered and that lowers your vibration. Maybe you have a habit of feeling abandoned, or unworthy, or fearful. If and when you get triggered into one of those patterns and you notice that your vibration is lower, choose to be kind and patient with yourself. You're learning and growing. So treat yourself in the same way you would treat a small child, with lots of love and compassion. Then next time you're in a similar situation with the opportunity to get triggered, to keep playing out a pattern, you can make a new choice that leads to you holding a steadier, higher vibration!
- Choose to focus your attention on things that make you feel good. This goes for news, TV shows, books, etc.
- Limit the time you spend on technological devices.

- Take frequent retreat days to release your "to-do list" and to be without an agenda or desire to "get somewhere".
- Call upon your guides, angels, and god in prayer to help you raise your vibration higher.

SPIRITUAL LOVE-MAKING

Chapter 31

Hello, friends. The channel has been in meditation, or as we call it, "sacred retreat." And thus he is feeling quite blissful. And so it is that as a reflection of the vibration that he cultivated in his sacred retreat, the chorus to a U2 song came into his awareness: "Ain't Love The Sweetest Thing." And so it is, friends, many of you are looking for love, yes? And many of you say, "I have not found it yet! I am still looking for it. I am still looking for 'the one'! Where is he? [or] Where is she? It is incredibly frustrating! I cannot find the right person."

We tell you that the love is inside of yourself. That is where it is. And it is not necessary to be with another to experience it. And yet, almost magically, one day it will arrive on your doorstep.

And you will see that the love you have found within yourself has appeared outside of yourself as well. And then you will both be in love together.

And your love will amplify and become even greater and more enjoyable. This is what we call a "sacred relationship," friends. And these are the relationships we wish all of you to have. Whether it lasts forever, or it only lasts a little bit of time, is irrelevant. Some of you will have one; others will have many. And that will be based partly on what you came here to experience, and partly by your programming, conditioning, and what feels comfortable for you.

And once you are in this sacred relationship, you will need to remember to allow yourself to be loved completely, so that you may experience how it feels to truly be loved by another person. And then the circle is complete, friends. You are in a state of love by yourself. And that love is returning to you and constantly filling you up with more and more love. How sweet is that?! We are laughing because we are circling back to the song title, yes? This is the experience of love that is available to all of you.

We are not discouraging you from taking any action that you feel is appropriate to find this particular person. But more likely than not, they will show up without much effort on your part because you are aligned vibrationally. And that will be that. And then you will spend as much time together, in love, as you are meant to. And if you are following our teachings, well then you will know that when it is time for the relationship to dissolve, you will let it go. Because as you know by now, it is easier to let go than to hold on. And holding on creates suffering that is unnecessary. And you will still be in love! Because you will not have lost the love that is inside of you. And so it is that somebody new will show up! And you will experience a sacred relationship with them!

Dear friends, perhaps we fooled you! Earlier in the book, we said there would be a chapter on spiritual love-making. Well this is it! This is not about the nuts and the bolts of it. It is not about how to do it physically. You can figure that out on your own. This is about coming into the vibration of love and then sharing that openly with a partner who is also in the vibration of love.

And then you will see that the act of love-making becomes much more of an energetic experience than a physical experience.

That is what most of you have become acclimated to based on what you see in cinema and advertisements. Well that is not it. That is not love-making, friends. We are not saying that it cannot be fun every once in a while. So if you would like to please yourself in that way, by all means. But we are saying that this is not spiritual love- making. Spiritual love-making is more energetic. Spiritual love-making is when you sit in the presence of someone in a state of love, allowing this vibration of love to guide you to an experience of love-making which leads to divine union. Here, there is no longer a "you," or "your partner," but only oneness, bliss, and ecstasy.

We are not going to share what the channel has or hasn't experienced in regards to this! This would be a little embarrassing for him. But he knows that what we speak of is available to him, although perhaps he has not experienced it yet, as we speak of it. But he has raised his vibration to a point where he is now available to experience it. And we hope, by way of our teachings, that you have as well, or at least you are in the process of doing so.

And so now you see, friends, why this particular transmission is coming now, towards the end of the book. It is impossible to experience spiritual love-making in a sacred relationship unless you have cultivated a state of love in your heart. It is that simple. And this love must be very pure, with very little ego attached to it, if you want to experience a sacred relationship in its highest form, yes?

Dear ones, once you are in a sacred relationship (and you will know when you are; you will not have to ask yourself if it is or not - you will know), then you might seek out a teacher who can guide you into this state of union of which we speak. We will tell you that the channel cannot be your teacher for this! He too will need a little bit of instruction. We are all laughing together now. So perhaps you will see him with a partner at a retreat, and you will be there with your partner as well. And you will look at each other and laugh. This is possible! It is very possible. You will say, "Oh, I have read your book!" And you will both have a good chuckle.

Dear friends, we want you to imagine a world in which all relationships are what we label as "sacred relationships." Can you imagine that? It would be quite amazing, no? There will be no room on the planet for wars. There will be too much love! And so it is, we honor all teachers on this planet guiding people back into their heart centers. And we honor all of the teachers on the planet for helping to facilitate the union of the spiritual woman and the spiritual man, or couplings of the same gender, so that there may be more peace and more love on the planet.

Now, you may be surprised that we are going to end this transmission by speaking about the children again! You might say, "Children? What are they doing here in this chapter?" We continue to laugh, friends. Everybody is in need of more of that. It is because the children have been misguided. They have little or no concept of what a sacred relationship is and the possibilities of what a sacred relationship can hold. And so, friends, there is nothing to be embarrassed about here. This needn't be a taboo subject on the planet anymore. It is time to gather the children when they are of age, and you will know what that age is. You will know intuitively when they are ready for this particular conversation. And heart to heart, you will share with them what a sacred relationship is, and the possibilities that it holds. And they will say, "Oh yes, that is what I want!" This very thing, making every relationship a sacred one, is part of heaven becoming manifest on this planet, friends.

Certainly, the consciousness of humanity has not risen to a point where all are ready for these types of relationships. But many of you are. And so it is that we share this very important teaching with you. It is just as important, if not more important, than the other teachings.

Dear friends, when two people come together, who are in a very high vibrational state of love, anything becomes possible. This is how planets are born, friends. This is how universes are made. This is how galaxies are birthed! And this is a path, friends, that will lead to the discovery of your own divinity in a new way that you have not experienced before.

We will leave with this, friends: be patient. If someone comes knocking on your door, you do not have to jump into bed with them simply because they look good, or because they made a funny joke, or because there is the possibility that they might take you on a nice vacation! From our perspective, it is better to cultivate the love in your own heart, until it has risen to a point where you are ready to attract the relationship you are meant to be in, the sacred relationship of which we speak. And we promise you that it will show up if you want it to show up! When you are truly ready for it to show up, it will show up! And when it is time to end the relationship, you needn't drag it out for weeks, or months, or sometimes even years because you are afraid of letting go, because you are afraid that perhaps nobody else will come into your life. They will, friends. They will.

And so now it is that we say our goodbyes for the evening and wish you all many blessings. Some of you are in a sacred relationship already but you do not even know it! So if that is you, and you know who you are, it is time for it to blossom. And we simply wish for all of you to hold the space for every being on this planet to express their sexuality in any way they please. We of course say this within the context that there must always be respect for the other person or other people who are involved. All boundaries must be respected, honored, and cherished. The man must honor and respect the woman. And the woman must honor and respect the man. And the same goes for same-gender couples. But remember to see all through the eyes of love, regardless of sexual preference or sexual taste, regardless of what somebody enjoys that you might not enjoy. Allow it all, friends.

*Celebrate your uniqueness in this way and
all shall be well on the planet.*

The channel is asking us about those who are incredibly closed-minded because they have been programmed and conditioned to believe something that is not the truth. And we say that if they are not doing physical harm to others, then to allow them to have their beliefs as well. And in time, their beliefs will no longer be their beliefs. They will open up to the truth as well. If not in this incarnation, then in another. So there is nothing to worry about. You do not need to impose your truth upon someone else. We will end with seven simple words that you already know to be true: love is love and that is that. Celebrate this, friends, yes? Love is love and that is that. Blessings, dear ones.

THE SACRED SPACE WITHIN YOU

Chapter 32

Good morning, friends. We are laughing with the channel. For he woke up to the sound of elephants outside of his apartment. We are not speaking of the literal kind, of course. We are speaking of a moving company who is moving somebody in or out of his building. And so it is that he was awakened quite abruptly! And just as most would do, his first thought upon waking was one of complaint, that he would have liked to have slept for a little bit longer. And so now he is sitting in his sacred retreat and allowing our words to flow through him for the benefit of all.

Dear friends, certainly there will be moments in your life that are not as pleasing to you as you would like them to be! And you might not have any control over what is happening around you. But what you always have control of is your state of being, yes? The channel was noticing that if he sat in his retreat and at the same time fought what was going on around him, this created more disharmony and not less. But when he chose to create space for what is, regardless of the sounds that were (and still are occurring) around him, he created more harmony for himself. So do you see friends, that if at times you choose the path of least resistance simply allow what is happening to happen, you can create a more harmonious experience for yourself?

By way of your sacred retreat practice, you do have control over how you are going to experience the moment.

And so now there is still quite a bit of noise outside, but the channel is feeling quite relaxed, quite at ease, and the contentment and the blissful feeling that he often feels in his sacred retreat is even beginning to settle in. And so what we are saying, friends, is that no matter what is happening around you, you do have quite a say in how you will experience it. And why not choose the path that will offer you the most harmony, yes? The most easefulness, yes? You needn't put on your boxing gloves and fight what you cannot fight. This is a simple teaching, friends, in allowing and creating space, yes? You will know when it is time to integrate this lesson into your life. You will have a moment, or perhaps you have had one or many already, in which you say to yourself, "Oh! This is that moment of which The Light Teachers were speaking, when I must integrate this teaching into my life and into my practice."

The channel certainly has his preferences, his likes and his dislikes. And certainly, he would much prefer these particular people to not be moving today. But yet by way of his spiritual practice, he is able to elevate enough to where it does not have such an impact on him and his vibration.

Do you now see the teaching, friends? It is all about empowerment, yes?

*It is about empowering yourself to experience as much peace
and contentment as you can in every moment of your life,
regardless of what is happening around you.*

And by way of your sacred retreat practice, it is very possible to rise enough to where you experience more of that peace and less of what it is that you say is being a nuisance in your life. And today in particular, we are speaking about the things that you cannot change. And on a deeper level, friends, this even extends to moments in which you are suffering physically.

Through your practice of sacred retreat, there is always an experience to be had that is elevated from what you might call your "normal" state of being. There is always an experience to be had in which you are feeling more peace, more contentment, and more acceptance. And as we said, you will know which moments are the ones of which we speak.

And so we will leave you with this, friends. Always do your best to stay high regardless of what is happening around you, yes? We have said this many times, in many different ways. Now we are just putting it in a different context. From our perspective, the power is within you to almost always stay high. And we throw the word "almost" in there only because we know that most of you, in your minds, cannot be in agreement without that word being included.

And there might come a time, friends, when you are having a particular life experience and where for a short period of time, you give up on staying high. This is not one of those.

*But almost always, the practice is to stay high. And you
do that through the practices that we have shared with you.
In particular, the practice of sacred retreat.*

And as we have said before, if you are not there yet, if you are not feeling elevated through this practice, then you need to practice more. Perhaps it is that you need to sit for longer periods of time. Perhaps it is that you need to sit more often, yes? So that, when you have an experience like the channel is having this morning, you can drop into the sacred space within, that space which is not impacted by what is going on around you.

And so it is, friends, we are going to invite the channel to call this chapter "The Sacred Space Within You," even though we have only mentioned those words once towards the very end of the chapter. This is the space we want you to access as often as possible. This is the space in which you are connected to your true self, which is peace and contentment; it is all that you are. Stay here, friends. This is what we are encouraging you to do. And you will see that by doing that, by staying in the sacred space that is within you, all will be well. The further away you stray from it, the more challenging your experience of life will be. The channel is realizing that when he strays a little bit farther away from it, he needs to sit for a little bit longer to get back in. This is the nature of things, friends. But we encourage you to forever and always stay with the practice that we have shared with you in this book.

*Let it be the one practice that you never give up on, that you stay
devoted to, no matter what is going on in your life.*

And by doing that, your experience of life will be dramatically transformed.

And so it is, friends, we are very content that we have been able to join you today to share this particular teaching with you. And we offer you many blessings for a harmonious day, during which you choose to stay in the sacred space within you as life continues to happen around you. Do you see, friends, that it does not happen to you? It happens around you. And you get to choose how you relate to it, either by getting all mixed up in it or by staying within yourself, by staying in the sacred space in your heart from which you are filled with everything that you want and everything that you need. There are many teachings in this particular transmission, friends. So re-read it.

We are going to let the channel go now. And we say to him that he is making progress, just as you are. For if it were earlier on in his spiritual path, he would have gotten up, he would have complained about the noise, and thus he would have said, "It is not a good day to practice sacred retreat." But no, he sat because this is his practice. And so he was able to elevate himself a little bit. He was able to retreat into the sacred space that is within him. And so now, friends, finally it is revealed why we call this practice "sacred retreat" and not "meditation."

You are retreating back into the sacred space that is within you.

You are retreating from what is around you, back into your heart of hearts where your god-self resides, where all is well now, and where all will be well forever and always. So it is that our teaching is to encourage you to be one with your god-self at all times, no matter what is happening around you.

We will leave you with this, friends. By committing to your practice of sacred retreat in all of life's situations, you will find that one day, you will be in a very stressful situation. You will be out of your element. You will be in a place of discomfort. You will not have access to your meditation cushion. And yet you will be able to sit, to close your eyes, and to drop right back into your god-self and to know that all is well because it cannot be any other way if you are in the sacred space that is within you. And it is by way of every sacred retreat that you have gone on, that you will have equipped yourself to do that. And now it is that we are complete. As we often do, we laugh. For as you know by now, it is a habit of ours to tell you that we are done, but to not be done. Blessings, friends.

LOVE IS THE ANSWER

Chapter 33

Good morning, friends. It is a great day to sit in your heart, is it not? For when you sit in your heart, your experience of life becomes incredibly pleasurable. And dear friends, you can not push yourself into your heart. You must relax into your heart. And so it is that sometimes it takes a little bit of time to relax. And thus, it might take a little bit of time to settle into your heart. But we tell you, friends, it is worth the conscious intention of doing so. For this is where the sweetness is found.

Do you see, friends, that there are some fruits you must peel to get to the good stuff inside? Yes? And so it is like this with your heart. It is inside of you. You must relax into it, so that you can experience it, so you can experience the pleasure that life has for you. We tell you that if you are not in your heart, it will not be that pleasurable. But if you are in your heart, it will be quite pleasurable indeed.

And we tell you, friends, that if you take the time to relax and to settle into your heart prior to reading our words, that even while you are reading our words, your experience will be very different. You will be much more open to receiving them, not only with your mind, but with your heart and your spirit. They will be easily digested. And they will have an energetic impact on your state of being. If you read our words in this way, your heart will open even more and you will receive even more. In fact, friends, we would encourage you not to read, but to simply receive. The words will make their way into your intellect, do not worry. But we encourage you to receive the words energetically.

As your heart blossoms, friends, your life will blossom as well!

It is like that. And so it is that we call ourselves The Teachers of The Light because we are teachers of the light. But you might also think of us as "teachers of the heart." For where there is light, there must be love. For light emanates from love. And this love that we speak of emanates from the source of creation and also emanates from your own heart. And so it is the very source of creation that resides within you, in your very own heart. That is quite delightful, is it not?

We do not want to say that it requires effort to settle into your heart and to experience this love of which we speak. But it does require intention. And it does require what we call "discipline." For you must be aware when you are not in your heart, so that you may settle back in. And this practice of sacred retreat that we have shared with you, is the best tool to cultivate this discipline. For by way of your sacred retreat, you are cultivating a heightened state of awareness that will begin to permeate every breath that you take.

And so it is that you might be sitting, or standing, or doing something in the middle of your day, and you might have the awareness that you are not settled into your heart. And then you will simply settle back in. And it will become easier and easier and easier to do this as you progress in your spiritual journey, with the teachings that we share with you. And in particular, your practice of sacred retreat.

You do not go into your practice of sacred retreat
just to come out unchanged.

Every time you go in, there is a little change which happens that allows you to experience the outside world a little bit differently. One day you will find, friends, that no matter where you are, no matter what it is you are doing, no matter who it is that you are surrounded by, that you are present forever and always in your heart, which is where the unconditional love of creator resides.

We do not like to use the word "goal," friends. But if there were a goal, that would be it, to be there in your heart space, all of the time.

As more and more people on your planet do this,
reside in their hearts all of the time, heaven will
become manifest on earth and that will be that.

For every thought and every action will come out of love. And when that happens, well, then you are living in paradise. And even when there is disagreement, it is resolved from a space of love. And thus everything is always returning to love, which is where it is meant to be.

We tell you this, friends: love is the answer. That is it. If someone is to ask you, "Tell me about your spiritual practice. Why do you do 'this'? Why do you do 'that'?" You tell them, "It is so that I may reside in my heart center and think and act out of love all of the time." And from our perspective, if you are participating in any spiritual group or any organized religion that does not have this simple goal, then we ask you: why are you there?

We encourage you to seek out community with those
who have the same goal that you do.

And if the community that you are part of does not share this interest, then you can practice on your own until you find the proper one. If you sit in community with others and do not feel drawn into your heart in the manner of which we are speaking, then we tell you that there is another community that will be better for you. And if you are told that a particular community is the one you are meant to be in, you must know that nobody can tell you that. Only your own heart can tell you that. Only your own inner guidance can tell you that. Do you see what we are getting at, friends?

If you enter into a community (specifically now, we speak of spiritual communities), and people are singing, and they are dancing, and they have big smiles on their faces, and you can tell right away that they are in their hearts, and that there is great love in the room, then this is a community that is worth exploring, yes? You will know, friends, if it is right for you or if it is wrong for you.

We will leave you with this, friends, because we think it is quite important. The channel, on a few occasions, attended a gathering of many people in what might be labeled as a "place of worship." But at this particular gathering, people of every color, people of every religion, people of every gender and everything in-between, and people of every sexual preference, were all there to celebrate together.

And in this particular room, there was the feeling of upliftment and of love. All were invited into this celebration. And the man who led these gatherings, who still leads them, only spoke of love. There were no rules and there was nothing ever said to infer that this was the only way and that no others were invited. And this particular gathering served the goal of which we speak, which is for every human being to be present in their hearts where the unconditional love of creator resides for all, always.

So friends, we encourage you to seek out gatherings like this one, where you will truly be uplifted, where there will truly be resonance in your heart of hearts. We are complete. We offer you many blessings, friends. You are great love. That is who you are. That is how we see you. By way of your practice, we encourage you to know yourself as we know you, as we see you, and nothing less, and to never put limitations on this love, to never say, "Yes, I will love this person but not that person." That is not love. That is what we would call a "limited form" of love. And we want you all to love expansively and unconditionally, for the benefit of all. Blessings, friends.

THE POWER WITHIN

Chapter 34

Are you beginning to see, friends, that there is great power within you? And how you feel, energetically speaking, is not dependent upon what is going on around you? For in the story of life, there will always be something going on around you, yes? Just as you might go to the cinema, yes? You get to watch it, and you get to participate in it, by giving it your attention. But it is only by way of your attention that you feel a particular way.

And so what we are encouraging you to do, friends, is to make it a priority to pay attention to yourself! And only then, open your eyes to see, and to participate in, the story that you would like to be involved in. When we ask you to pay attention to yourself, as your number one priority, we are asking you to tend to the garden of your own heart. And in this way, you determine how you feel energetically. Life does not determine that. You determine that!

And this is what we mean when we say that you have great power within you to consciously choose how you are going to feel during this life experience.

The practice that we have given you for doing this is very simple because it needn't be complicated. It is to sit as often as needed, and for as long as needed, until you unplug from the story that is going on around you. And as you unplug from that, you plug into yourself. You plug into the great peace that is within you. You plug into the great love that is within you. You raise your vibration. You begin to smile more often. You begin to experience more joy in your heart. And then you will see the story that is going on around you will change. The movie that you have been watching, and that you have been participating in, will change. It will change to reflect all of these new feelings that you are experiencing, just by sitting. This is what we call the "law of attraction in action."

Do you see, friends, that you put the law of attraction into action, not through action, but by sitting and paying attention to yourself, and making that your number one priority? Do you see, friends, that you do not jump out of bed, open your eyes, and begin to observe and participate in the story that is going on around you? You can if you want to. But that is not our recommendation. The story that you are observing and participating in will become much more pleasurable if instead, you get out of bed, you sit, and you experience sacred retreat.

And you do that, as often as you need to during the day, for as long as you need to, to plug back into your real self. So this is the teaching today, friends. What you see, what you participate in outside of yourself, what you might call your "story," is not as real as you think it is. It is passing by like clouds in the sky. So how real can it be? From our perspective, that which is real and true is what you plug into when you close your eyes and you go within. And it is all that we have spoken of already in this particular teaching and in others as well.

It is great peace. It is serenity. It is bliss. It is contentment.
It is satisfaction. It is all that you are, friends.

Put your attention on this, and from that space, once you have found all of this inside of yourself, only then do we encourage you to observe the story and to participate in it. And to enjoy it, friends! That is what you are here to do. You are here to enjoy life, right? You are here to enjoy the story of life. You are here to enjoy observing it. You are here to enjoy participating in it. That is why you are here, yes? Why else would you have come?

It is meant to be an enjoyable life experience. You are meant to have an enjoyable experience, while both observing and participating. You are meant to meet many characters who you enjoy spending time with, and who you create magnificent things with that will impact the lives of others in a beneficial way. And thus you are fulfilling your soul purpose of which we have already spoken about in this book. And then when you leave your body, your consciousness and your awareness will look back and say, "Wow, that was an enjoyable life. And it was enjoyable because I created it to be so by going within first, by discovering what is within me first, and allowing my life to be a reflection of that."

Do you see how everything works, friends? Are you beginning to see it now? Are you beginning to see that you are the projector that projects the movie out onto the screen? We are talking about the movie of your life. We tell you, that what you project can be truly miraculous.

*What you project can be quite splendid if you choose to make it
your priority to place your attention on what is within you first.*

And then you will see that things will begin to shift, little by little.

It does not mean you wake up and everything has changed around
you. Although sometimes it could be that way. But more often than
not, little by little, things shift. You begin to observe and participate
in new scenes. You meet new characters that are reflective of the new
high vibration which you have cultivated by way of your sacred
retreat. And by way of your sacred retreat, friends, you begin to feel
inspired to take action in a harmonious way so that you become a co-
creator in the universe.

So do you see, friends, that we are not telling you to not take action
in your life? We are not telling you to just sit. We are telling you to do
that (sit), but we are also telling you to take inspired action. You
might be asking yourself, "What is it? What is inspired action?" And
so here's what we are going to tell you friends:

*Inspired action is when you open your eyes after your
sacred retreat, and you have a sense that you should
take a particular action in your life.*

This is your spirit speaking to you. It is not your mind telling you to
do this or to that. It is your spirit that is leading you onwards, yes? For
your spirit might know the destination that is reflective of the new
high vibration that you are cultivating by way of your sacred retreat.
And so it is that your spirit will lead you there if you listen. And your
spirit will inspire you to take action that leads you to this destination.
But by way of your high vibration, you will enjoy every moment of it,

you will enjoy every moment of the journey, yes? For that is what it is about.

If our consciousness serves us correctly, we are quite certain we have spoken about this in a different way. And if we have not yet, then we are about to. We say that it is by your inspired action, that things begin to shift more quickly, yes? And it is by way of your new high vibration that things simply begin to show up, mysteriously and magically. And then you might find yourself participating in life in a new, unexpected, joyful way.

Do you know, friends, how it is that the channel does what he is doing right now? It is by way of his sacred retreat. He does not just sit and channel. We share this with you, friends, because he did not know that he would be doing this. But it is by way of his sacred retreat that it came to be. It is by way of his sacred retreat that it became possible. And so we would say, friends, quite boldly, that many of the highest possibilities that exist for you and your life can and will unfold if you go within first, and make it your practice to do that.

And you will see too, friends, that by way of your sacred retreat, what we might call your "human traits," which are quite adept at getting in the way of you stepping forward fully on your path, will begin to dissolve. We are speaking of the feeling of fear and self-doubt. For these are two things that have cycled quite regularly, in and out for much of the channel's life. And so it is there has been a lot of stopping and starting for the channel. Do you see what we mean, friends? There is the starting, then there is the fear and the doubt, and then there is the stopping. But as a result of the sacred retreat practice, much of the fear that he picked up in his childhood, that he carried with him into his adulthood, is finally beginning to dissolve and to simply disappear. And it is like this as well for the self-doubt that has also caused him to start and to stop, and to start and to stop.

We share this with you, friends, because we want you to know about the power that the practice of sacred retreat holds. It can support you in many ways, not just in the way that we have spoken of in this particular chapter. And the channel does not mind us sharing what has made him human, as long as it serves to teach others. And he has raised his vibration to the point now where there is little judgment. Do you see what we mean by that, friends? He does not moan to himself, "Oh, I have started and stopped so many times. If I hadn't done that, I could've been living this (a different) life right now." This is something he did quite a bit when he was just a little bit younger. But now most of the time, he is simply present with the possibilities that exist in the moment for him, with little fear and little doubt. And that is why we are expecting that his life is going to flourish and bloom in unexpected ways in a very short period of time. Again we share this with you, friends, so that you know where this practice of sacred retreat can take you.

We share this with you so you know the power of transformation that is inherent in the practice of sacred retreat… so that you know what is possible.

The channel has no problem with us sharing where he has been, vibrationally speaking, and where he is now. There were times when he was very low vibrationally. He would complain most of the time. He was depressed sometimes. He was stagnant most of the time. He was fearful quite a bit of the time. And he was in self-doubt much of the time. He is laughing! But most of that is behind him now, and it is because he has plugged himself into his true self, to the great peace, and to the great love that is within him. And we ask you to do the same so that you may be transformed as well.

And we tell you, friends, that there is always a higher level of consciousness and a higher vibration for you to experience. If you say to yourself, "Oh, I am quite high already. My life is quite divine already," that is good. But we say there is more for you to experience by going within, and that it will literally turn your world upside down. Because you will come to know who you really are! We are going to leave you with that, friends. Even though it is a bit mysterious.

As we often do, friends, even though there might be a very simple title to the chapter, we have spoken of many things in this transmission. There are many teachings that are contained within it. And so we encourage you to read it again, and to read it as we have instructed you to do so, by relaxing into it, by softening into it, and by allowing yourself to receive the vibration that is inherent in the words rather than simply reading them as if you were reading a novel. For these words were not meant to be read like that.

We will say they were meant to be read with
your heart and your spirit.

And though it is by way of your eyes that you are doing so, your eyes are simply present to allow your heart and your spirit to receive. Is this not the way it really should be every time your eyes are open? We wish you many blessings as you celebrate this day in which you have the privilege to witness and participate. And we wish you many blessings as that which you are observing and participating in continues to shift, mirroring the vibration you connect with during your sacred retreat. Blessings, dear ones.

ENDLESS LOVE

Chapter 35

Dear friends, as we have said, we are here to do our best to honor the entire human life experience. And so it is if you are grieving the loss of somebody that you love, or something traumatic has happened, we are not going to encourage you to sit and raise your vibration. Instead, we would encourage you to simply allow yourself to feel however it is you are feeling.

Do you see, friends, that the word "emotion" is meant to be divided into "e-motion"? It is energy in motion, yes? And so you must let that energy move and release through you so that you might feel light again. The only thing we would discourage you from is to make it a habit. Do you see what we are saying, friends? There are some that grieve and it becomes a habit, rather than something they move through.

So take the necessary time to allow whatever it is you are feeling to flow through you.

Much in the way that a river might flow,
allow the energy to flow through you.

But very quickly friends, without delay, we encourage you to return to the practices that we have outlined for you in this book, in particular the practice of sacred retreat. And then, to once again raise your vibration back up to where it belongs. For you were not meant to grieve for very long.

And when we speak of grieving, we do not only mean the departure of a loved one, but we speak of any particular life experience that might cause you to grieve or to experience a very heavy emotion. But do not let it be for long, friends! Because you are here to have an enjoyable life experience, right? And so one morning you will wake up and your intuition will speak to you. It will say, "Okay, now is the time to let this experience go and to move back into a new experience of joy."

The channel was watching a documentary the other day about a particular tribe in Africa where the men are required to wear the same clothing for six months without a shower after the departure of a loved one. We are not here to disrespect any traditions. But from our perspective, that is not necessary. Allow the energy to flow through you. And then return to your practice of raising your vibration, moving into your heart-center, and experiencing the joy of your being. And then allow that joy you have found within yourself to be reflected by the universe that is here to please you and to give you many wonderful experiences of life.

From our perspective, friends, if you are flying high above the clouds, as we hope you often do, enjoying your experience of life, and something traumatic occurs that leaves you below the clouds caught in the rain, remember that you are not meant to stay there for very long.

You are meant to rise, rise, rise back above the clouds.
You are meant to fly high again.

So if that short period of time begins to extend itself, we encourage you to return to every other practice that we have shared with you in this book and to elevate yourself back into your rightful place, with creator, with us, and the high vibration of love, where you are meant to reside as often as possible. And remember, friends, love has no end. This is very important. The forms that you love may change. But the love that you have inside of yourself, for what was contained within the form, never has to end.

We are speaking in particular to the experience of death, yes? Let your love continue. There needn't be any real loss. For in reality, from our perspective, you are not losing anything at all. The love remains and the love continues. And so some of you might experience what others consider to be a great loss in their lives. But you will simply have great love in your heart.

And there will be no grieving at all because there will be nothing at all
to grieve from where you are situated, vibrationally speaking.

There is no right or wrong path to take, friends. But we say that both paths lead to the same destination, which is a place of endless love that continues for all of eternity. So focus on that, friends. Stay in love, yes? Stay in love with every form that you have ever met on this planet. And focus on that rather than the loss which, from our perspective, is an illusion. For you cannot lose love. It cannot be lost. And the spirit, the god-self that is contained within every form on this planet, cannot be lost. That is eternal, friends. Only the form taken by god's presence is temporary.

And so it is, you see, that there are multiple teachings in this transmission as well, as there have been in many. So if you need to re-read it, do that. Our love for you, friends, will never change. It does not matter what form you are in!

And though we have great love for you in this particular form now, when you are in a different form, we will love you the same.

And we will not experience the loss of you. There will be no loss.

So do you see, friends, that we have offered you two different perspectives? And we say that if the experience of loss is part of your path, and the emotional experience that comes with that, it is perfectly fine. And if you only are to experience endless love without any loss at all, that is good as well. And in this way, we are honoring both the human experience and what we might label as the "higher teachings." For that is what the channel has asked us to do, so that our teachings are complete.

So with that said, with great love in our hearts, we offer you many blessings for a day that is filled with great love. For that is who you are. And that love can never be taken away from you. Read that sentence again friends: For that is who you are. And that love can never be taken away from you. Perhaps many times in your life, you thought that love was being taken away from you. But it never has, because it is inside of you. It is kind of a riddle, yes? But it is not meant to be that way. It is meant to be a very simple, direct teaching. So we are very pleased that you are receiving it in the way that you are. And that is it, friends.

BIG VIBRATIONAL SHIFTS

Chapter 36

There are some of you reading these words, and you know who you are, who are going through very big changes in your lives, yes? In fact, you might even say there is an upheaval taking place. We tell you, friends, that if you are on a spiritual path, one that is leading you to the experience of greater freedom and greater joy in your life, it is only natural that this might occur in your life.

One way to put it, friends, is that if you are committed to moving forward along your path in life, there is some stripping away that must occur at the same time. The channel is experiencing quite a bit of this right now. He is experiencing it on a physical level. For physically, he is in quite a bit of pain as he allows himself to carry this transmission forward for you this evening. We tell him that there is a purpose to whatever it is he is experiencing physically right now.

So friends, if you are having one of these experiences, and it might not necessarily be a physical experience, it might be showing up somewhere else in your life, you will know if it is an experience you are having because there is a higher purpose to it. And that higher purpose is that you are moving forward along your path.

*And so it is, there is a shift that is occurring for you on
many different levels so that you may live the greatest,
most expansive life you came here to live.*

It is natural, friends, that the ego, as it is doing quite a bit with the channel, will rebel, yes? It will say, "It is very unpleasant. It is very unfair. I do not like it." But on a deeper level, your soul will know there is a purpose to what it is you are experiencing. During these times of great transition, friends, we encourage you to sit for long periods of time and to settle into whatever it is that is happening with acceptance. And trust that you are moving toward something. And when we say "something," we infer that you are moving toward a more expansive life that will be filled with more freedom and more joy.

Dear friends, we want you to know that we are pointing toward very specific experiences in your life that are related to this topic of which we speak. Do you see? It is when you know that something big is happening, that there is a shift that is occurring. You might equate it to an earthquake. Now do you see what we mean? We have used the word "vibration" quite a bit so we will use it again here. It means that you are shifting vibrationally very quickly in a short period of time.

That one sentence that we have just stated sums it up quite well, friends: It means that you are shifting vibrationally very quickly in a short period of time. And you will know if it is that kind of shift that is occurring in your life, yes? There will be an inner-knowing. It will not come from your mind because your mind cannot make sense of it. But your soul can. Your soul knows. And so that's why we say it is an "inner-knowing."

It means you are on your path, friends.

We know it might be difficult for you to celebrate that, right? But we still encourage you to do so. Or to at least embrace the change, to accept it, and to know that the upheaval will not last. It is only temporary. An earthquake does not last forever, does it? The earth shakes for a short period of time and then it stops. We are speaking of a change like this. The channel is going through one right now. And we will simply say that he is going through it so he can be of more service to others in his life.

So we say, friends, to accept the big shifts that are occurring in your life. This is the time, friends, for big shifts. Many are going through them. Often when awakening, there are big shifts. It is simply the nature of awakening. You might be going along quite easefully for a period of time. Then there will be a big shift. It is meant to take you into a more expansive life. And then when you look back, friends, you will have even greater clarity as to why it had to happen. As it is happening, your ego might not have that clarity! But your soul already does. As you progress forward along your path following the shift, your mind will catch up as well.

Because you will find yourself doing something you never would have done, if not for that shift. You will have an experience you never would have had if not for that shift.

This particular transmission, we say that it will not speak to everybody. But it is still to be included because it is likely it will speak to some of you. And it will actually be very beneficial for some of you. It will help you to make sense of what is happening in your life. You will read these words and you will say to yourself, "Oh yes, that is me! I am one of the ones who is having a big vibrational shift!" And we tell you, friends, that there are many others like you who are also experiencing big vibrational shifts right now. And that is it for today, friends.

PRACTICE & REFLECT WITH DARREN

Appreciation

As I sat in meditation this morning, I was guided to share this as the last practice that comes directly from me. It is the practice of appreciation. When you sit for sacred retreat, do more than just sit. Notice your breath, with the intention of settling into your heart. Be appreciative. Bring a sense of appreciation to the fact that you are breathing and have been blessed with a human incarnation.

I invite you to bring this sense of appreciation not only to your practice, but to each and every moment of life. Give thanks for your body. Give thanks for the food you eat. Give thanks for the water you drink. Give thanks for the freedom you have to practice sacred retreat. Give thanks for your friends. Give thanks for your family, even if some of your familial relationships are challenging. And give lots of thanks and love back to Mother Earth.

Know that from every challenging experience, there is something to be gained that can point you toward a new, more enjoyable life experience if you are willing to be honest with yourself, learn, and grow. Rather than getting stuck in the mud with the lower vibrations of fear, anger, and resentment towards yourself and others, choose the higher path. Put a smile on your face, be grateful for the lessons, and move on. Practice sacred retreat every day and make it your intention to keep raising your vibration in love and appreciation.

In a sense, life is all about letting go. We let go of each and every breath so we can inhale another. Every moment is like a mala bead on a string of mala beads. The string, the thread that unites all the beads, is the thread of appreciation. At first, appreciation might need to be a little forced. Perhaps you should consider making a list, for instance, of what you're grateful for every day. But with a strong and consistent sacred retreat practice, you will find yourself more centered in your heart. This will lead to a natural way of being, where appreciation becomes second nature. And it needn't take a tragedy or great loss to make you more grateful for life. You can start now, today.

YOUR "TO-DO" LIST

Chapter 37

Good morning, friends. From our perspective, friends, no matter what it is that you have to do on your "to-do" list, there is nothing that should take priority over sitting for as long as you need to sit, to still your mind and to tune back into your heart center.

Do you remember the transmission in which we spoke of tuning the heart much like you would tune an instrument? It is quite easy to go out of tune when you are outwardly focused. So we want to make this very important distinction today, friends. It is a distinction between being outwardly focused and tuning into the great love and great light within you, thus being inwardly focused. You already know which feels better, don't you? For it is an experience, yes?

And by way of your sacred retreat, it feels quite delightful to be inwardly focused.

And it can feel quite disharmonious, and out of tune, if you are outwardly focused all of the time. There must be a balance, friends.

If this practice of tuning we have spoken of earlier is not part of your life, then it is only natural that you will feel overwhelmed by your "to-do" list. Your experience of life will not be harmonious because you will, more often than not, be outwardly focused. You might say to yourselves, "Oh, no, here we go again! The Light Teachers are going to speak about the importance of sacred retreat and going within." And yes we are, friends. But in a different way and in a different context.

We are going to get straight to the point, friends. When you are centered within yourself, when you are sitting in the seat of your soul, when you are in your heart, then all is well, is it not? For you might even say that you are on vacation from the outside world when you are doing this! And that is why all is well. We say it is not because you are on vacation, but because you are home, where you are meant to be, energetically speaking.

So do you see, friends, that if you come towards life from within yourself, that your experience of it will be much more easeful?

It will be much more relaxed. Whatever needs to get done can get done in a more easeful way, without the stress of feeling overwhelmed.

This is the gift, friends, that sacred retreat gives you. This is the gift that raising your vibration gives you. This is the gift that raising your level of consciousness gives you. This is the gift that coming to know yourself for who you are gives you. This is the gift that coming to know the great love and the great light that is within you gives you. This is the gift that coming to know the truth of your own being gives you. This is the gift that sitting in harmony with your god-self gives you.

Do you see friends, when you are experiencing all of that, which is well within your capacity to do, then everything changes? So you might open your eyes, and you might now be in that space of which we speak. And your "to-do" list is still the same. But we tell you, it will not be nearly as overwhelming. And in this way, you are bringing more balance into your life. And from this new perspective that you are in, as you stay at home, within yourself, you might even see that there are things on your "to-do" list that are not even necessary to do! You might see there are things that are not really a priority. You might see there are things that no longer interest you and are a waste of time.

We are just sharing some possibilities with you that might come up as you continue to rise, rise, rise and take this sacred journey with us that we have invited you on. For some of you, this teaching might not make logical sense. It will only make sense when you have experienced what we want you to experience, and what is available for all of you to experience by way of going within.

We tell you, friends, not to boast on behalf of the channel, but he went to bed and his mind was full of things to do. And he got up, and his mind was full of things to do. And in between, he awoke multiple times and his mind was full of things to do. And upon getting up, if he had tackled his list, he would have experienced a day that would not have been to his liking. It would have been full of struggle. It would have been full of dis-ease. He would have felt out of ease. But because it is his priority to sit, and to go within, and to allow the bliss of his being to surface and put a smile on his face, when he does open his eyes again, and this transmission is over, energetically everything will have shifted and he will have a much different experience of his day. And it is not even that what is on his "to-do" list has changed. It is simply that *he* has changed! As you might remember, we mentioned that you bring your own personal vibration to every moment of your life experience. And thus your experience of life changes in every way.

When you elevate yourself, everything changes.
And the power is within you to do that!

The channel has just completed an advanced life coach training program so that he can be of service to others in a more powerful way. And in his last class, a woman was being coached. And she said, "Oh, I am so busy. I am so stressed. And I have no time for anything I want to do!" This is the case with most of humanity, yes? And the session ended with a plan of attack on how to deal with that! Our plan of attack would have been for her to go on sacred retreat for at least thirty minutes twice a day. And to that she might have said, "I cannot do that! I already do not have enough time to do what I need to do!" But we tell you that if she were to do this, she would create an energetic shift. And that energetic shift would allow her to bring herself to each and every moment of life in a different way. And thus, she would experience less stress and more ease. Some of her "to-do" list would drop away. And no matter how much was on it, she would not feel as overwhelmed about it. And so this is the gift we are giving you today, friends. It is another reason why it is so incredibly important to practice sacred retreat.

Dear friends, we will leave you with this. You have to dive deep into the ocean to get to the pearl, correct? It lies on the ocean floor, yes? Sacred retreat is like this. You must allow yourself to settle beneath the surface of what is happening around you. You must allow yourself to *relax* beneath the surface of what is happening around you. You must allow yourself to *soften* beneath the surface of what is happening around you. And this includes your own thoughts as well.

> *Your thoughts are not happening within you.*
> *We see them as going on around you!*

And when you allow yourself to continue to settle deeper and deeper beneath the waves of the ocean, so to speak, what you will find is truly spectacular. It is beyond words! And every time you go on your sacred retreat, as we have shared already, you bring a little bit of it out with you. So when you open your eyes, and you participate in your day, you will be more settled than you had been prior! And thus your experience of life changes. And because you are raising your vibration, you attract new positive experiences into your life as well.

So please, friends, make this your priority. It will be well worth your while. Once you taste the sweetness of what we are offering you, you will understand. All we can do now is entice you to the point where you are curious enough to choose to take the journey with us. And we tell you that if you do, you will be well-rewarded. And we tell you that the reward you receive will be greater than any material award you could ever receive. We are complete, friends. As usual, we have given you many teachings in this transmission. And so we encourage you to reread it. Blessings, friends.

THE UNIVERSE RESPONDS TO YOU

Chapter 38

Good morning, friends. It is with great pleasure and with great joy that we speak to you today. For that is where our vibration is at the moment. And so it is we might ask you, where is *your* vibration? Are you vibrating with the frequency of pleasure and joy as well? And if not, then the answer is that you need to sit for as long as you need to settle into it. For we remind you, that it is within you, not outside of you.

Now do you see, friends, that the universe was put in place by creator to respond to your vibration? The channel is just beginning to get it. He does not quite believe it yet. Often his ego would like to tell him otherwise. But then he might have an experience that leads him to the knowingness that what we say is true. And he can only have this experience if he goes within, raises his vibration, and then allows the universe to respond to that.

So rather than trying to shape and mold the universe, we encourage you to allow the universe to respond to you. And it will, friends. Creating in this manner is much more pleasurable than the way many of you are used to, yes?

*You can sit back and allow things to happen simply
because of how high you are vibrating.*

Then miracles appear in your life instantaneously. The channel experienced one yesterday. He found himself at the perfect place, at the perfect time, to meet somebody that he was meant to meet. It came to be because of his intention and because of his vibration. And the universe responded to that. Do you see what we mean, friends? He did not run around asking everybody, "Are you the person I am meant to meet?" He simply went about his business with his intention being broadcast into the universe, his high vibration calling the right experience towards him. And then he collided with it in a very harmonious and pleasurable way. This is the path of creation that we wish you to take, friends. You can sit back, you can relax, and create all at the same time, friends. And creating in this way can be very pleasurable.

The channel wishes us to tell you that there will be a time for action. And your action is meant to support your intention and your high vibration. Do you see how it goes? Your action is there to support that. But even so, you can take action in a relaxed way. It does not have to be pushing and fighting.

*Dear friends, when you have a strong intention and you let the
universe know what this intention is, and you carry a high-vibration
with you everywhere you go, and you take inspired action whenever
you know it is truly needed, that truly is how you create.*

That is how you create your masterpiece. The channel is still learning. But he is getting better at it.

Do not get frustrated, friends. Just because something does not show up the moment you begin to think about it, does not mean it will not. It will. Do you see, friends, that if you become frustrated or agitated because what you want to show up is not showing up yet, then you will experience these negative emotions? And thus, the creative process will not be very enjoyable. But if you trust and allow things to happen in divine timing, without allowing your ego (and its judgments) to become involved, then all will be well. So when the ego begins to make judgment, smile at it! And then let it go very quickly. Tend to your vibration. Continue to tend to raising your vibration. Remind yourself of your intention. Have faith. Trust that the universe is in place to give you pleasure. And it will if you allow it to happen.

We are laughing. The channel is very adamant about us saying, "Oh, but yes, there is some action that will be required!" And we say that when it is time for that, do it in a relaxed and easeful way. And let your experience of creating be a joyful and harmonious one. This is the way it is meant to be. It is not meant to be a struggle, friends. Many of you see creation like that. But it is not meant to be like that. It is your programming and conditioning which says that.

The higher you rise, the easier it will become. You will see. This is a very advanced teaching, friends. Do not take it to be more of the same simple law of attraction that you might have read in the past. Re-read it.

Tune into the vibration that we are expressing through our words.
For the vibration that we share is here to support you in raising your
vibration, and thus experiencing all that you are meant to experience.

Stay relaxed, friends. Enjoy the journey that you are on. Look to the future if you may, toward all the pleasure that is about to come into your life. But stay present. And stay relaxed. There is never any need to get ahead of yourself. This will only create more struggle.

And so it is, friends, that we wish you a glorious day! One in which the cosmic sun shines upon you with all of her love, all of her light, and all of her warmth radiating through you. And we encourage you to stay in a state of allowance, receptivity, relaxation, and ease. All that you want and all that you need will be given to you because the universe is responding to your intention, your vibration, and to any inspired action you are taking that supports your intention. Blessings, friends.

BE HERE NOW

Chapter 39

Good morning, friends. We would like to begin by asking some questions: Are you present? Are you present in the moment in which your body is sitting or standing? Or is your mind drifting? If it is, we encourage you to *re-present* yourself! Ah, we are laughing. Re-present yourself by becoming present once again in the very moment in which you find yourself. For that is always where you are meant to be.

You are never meant to be anywhere else but the present.

Do you see, friends, that all of creation takes place from the present moment, does it not? It cannot take place from the past or in the future. It must take place now, from the moment that is at hand.

Now we will ask you: Are you relaxed as well? If you are present but are not relaxed, then you are not as present as you can be. And it could be that you need to do something to relax your physical body. Perhaps you need to go do some yoga. Or perhaps you need to go dance or whatever it is that you do to relax your physical body.

The practice of sacred retreat, which we have spoken of so often, cannot take place in the way it is meant to if you are not fully relaxed.

That is to say you will not be able to settle as deeply into your heart as is possible if you are not very relaxed.

It is only when the channel is very relaxed that these words can flow freely through him. And if he is not, his lack of relaxation will serve as an obstacle to the flow of energy.

When you are present, friends, when you are relaxed, you have access to your heart, yes? And every teaching of ours is a teaching that is meant to guide you back to that place. Dear ones, we tell you that it is a very pleasurable experience to be present, to be relaxed, and to be in your heart. And it is from there that you may go out into the world and create your masterpiece, whatever it is you wish to create!

There have been times when the channel has said to himself, "Oh, this is all an illusion. I must escape. I must ascend." What we say is that while it is temporary, while it is a temporary expression, we encourage you to create within it, and to participate fully in it from a state of presence and deep relaxation, and most importantly, from a space of your heart! If your desire is flowing out of that, then it will feel quite delicious to you.

Another way to put it would be to say that the desire is flowing from within you, that it is bubbling up from within yourself, and that 'self' is resting in a state of peace, in a state of calm presence. And this is how we wish you to create. This is where we would like your desire to come from rather, for example, than looking around you and saying to yourself, "Oh wow, look at that person! Look at what they are doing! I am so envious! I wish I was like them!" That is not desire, friends. That is comparison, which creates struggle. Do you see the difference? We know you do. So we say good, let your desire guide you friends, yes? Let it guide your actions.

But always stay present, always stay relaxed, and
always stay in your heart, friends.

There is a teacher of the channel who once said that "love is your default setting." So this too is your default setting, yes? This state of deep peace, deep relaxation, and heart-centered presence. And from there, let your desire guide you forward, yes? And let it be the desire that matches up with your purpose for being on the planet. You will know if it is or if it is not, yes? If it is not, it might feel a little bit "off" to you. Let your desire be guided by your purpose for being here at this historic time of awakening for humanity. If you are not following that, then you are being of disservice to not only yourself, but to all of your soul brothers and soul sisters who are on the planet as well. For they need you! They need you to be in this default setting of which we speak! And they need you to follow desires that align with your soul purpose.

All of you who are reading these words are serving a very important role in the evolution of the planet. Allow yourself to feel that truth. That is the truth that we wish you to know today.

And we wish you to feel this truth experientially in your spirit
so that when you close the book, you feel inspired because you
know that you are here to serve a purpose on the planet.

If you allow yourself to stay in this default setting, if you allow your desire to guide you, then you will serve your purpose, correct? And when it is time to go, when you have fulfilled your purpose, then you will go. Then your spirit will continue its journey and leave the physical body behind. But for now, you are here! Are you not? Are you not sitting or standing wherever you are... reading these words... feeling the energy that we are transmitting today? Are you not alive? We are quite certain you are! So allow yourselves to be here, yes?

There is a very famous book called *Be Here Now* by a teacher by the name of Ram Dass. He is no longer in physical form, but his presence remains here for all to connect to and learn from. He is of particular interest for the channel because he is related to the practice of Bhakti yoga, the yoga of love and devotion, which the channel enjoys practicing as a musician. These are good words, friends: "be here now." But we would encourage you to create a little bit of a separation between the first two words and the third. "Be here…(because that is where you are)…now."

Now is the time. Now is the time to return to your default setting, to follow the desire that matches up to your purpose for being here on the planet. You can then contribute to this great awakening in the way in which you were meant to. We do not want to sound like a Nike commercial. But we say "just do it now." Contribute now. Return to your default setting. Settle within yourself. And then allow your desire to guide you.

The channel is beginning to do this. It has not come easily for him. Very often he follows it for a short period of time. And so now, just as we are encouraging him, we urge you to return to and stay in your default setting, continuing to follow your desire! Allow it to propel you like a rocket ship. Not so that you may fulfill the selfish desires of the ego. Because that is a different thing. We do not want you to do that. But rather so you can follow the desires of your heart which are related to your purpose for being here on the planet during this historic time of awakening.

We know we have said it already. But it must be quite important since we are saying it again! Yes, it must be! This is an important message for both yourselves and the channel. Feel the energy that is part of it. It is more than just words, friends. It is energy, yes? It is meant to uplift you. It is meant to inspire you, so that when you close this chapter, you know where you are going! We do not speak of a destination. No, not at all. Get it out of your heads that you are going to a particular destination in life. You are not.

There is no destination to be found, friends. There is no better tomorrow. There might be, but it is not the right mentality to have. There is only the possibility that exists in the present moment of your vibration. The mentality that you are continuously striving to get to the next destination is nonsense.

There is only now, friends.

And yet we tell you that this "now" you find yourselves in can take you to magical experiences that are beyond your wildest dreams. So that is where you are going! Let that be enough today, yes? You do not need to know exactly what that experience will be, who it will be with, where it will be, or when it will happen! You do not need to know any of that. That will put you into your head. And it will put you into a state of striving toward some future event that takes you out of the present moment. We do believe that we have made our point, yes? And we know that many of you get it. You get what we are saying. You are saying to yourselves, "Yes, that is it! I get it: Be here – Now." That is it for today.

YOU ARE LOVED

Chapter 40

Good morning, friends. We are settling in with the channel, energetically speaking. And as we do that, he is feeling the great love we have for him.

It was quite recently that he was feeling rather alone. He was feeling the void of this love that we and the supreme creator him-herself, has for him. In fact, he was in such a state of separation that he began to cry quite profusely. You might even say that he was crying to god. "Why am I so alone? Why doesn't anybody love me?" Do you see, friends, that in this particular moment, he was experiencing a great separation from who he is? That is not meant to be a riddle, friends, though you might think it is. For do you see, friends, that when you are settled into the truth of who it is you are, you will feel the opposite of being alone?

You will feel the great love that arises from within you, that is you!

And you will feel the great love that the universe, that your "invisible friends," as the channel likes to call them sometimes, and that the creator him-herself, has for you!

And so dear friends, if you are feeling isolated and you are feeling alone, and you need to cry, then do it. It is okay! But then let that moment go. And tune back into the love and the greatness that is within you. And allow yourself to be loved by all those who wish to love you. Be receptive to their love. Let the love in, friends. We are speaking of love that comes from both people and pets, as well as us here in the spirit world.

There is great love that is had for all of you.

There are some of you, the channel himself included sometimes, that think to yourselves, "I am very different. I cannot connect with people in the way that I wish to. And thus I feel isolated and alone." Well, we have given you the prescription, right? We have given you the remedy for this situation, have we not? But we will give you one more as well. You may pray for what the channel calls "sacred friendships" or "sacred connections" to come into your life. And they will, friends. They will. They will. They will. It could be that they come in very quickly. Or it could be that it takes a little bit of time for the right people to come into your life, the ones who you feel a resonance with, the ones you enjoy spending time with, the ones who uplift you, the ones who give you a sense that you are living in a community of people who truly love you and care about you. These people will come into your life as you continue to raise your vibration, and as you continue to call them in through your prayers and through the work you are doing on the planet. And that is that.

So do you know, friends, that there is great love that is within you that can be felt and experienced? This love, friends, is your birthright! It is not something you even need to seek, so to speak. For it is within you. It is not without.

And we say that when you connect to this, to the great love and the great light that is within you, that we have for you, it will be reflected in the people who come into your life as well.

And suddenly you will find that there are many people in your life who are very loving and who you feel great kinship with, who feel like your family. This is incredibly important for many of you who feel like you do not get along well with your blood relatives. So know that you all have a family. And if you are not surrounded by them right now, you will be soon, simply by following the practices that we have shared with you in this transmission, yes?

It is okay, friends, to feel your humanness every now and then. But then to know that your humanness is a very small part of who you are! That you are a spiritual being. That you are a vibrational being. And there is great power within you to uplift yourself, to feel the great love and the great light that is within you and is available for you to receive and experience in many different ways and in many different forms on this planet. This is our teaching for today, friends. Please know that we have great love for you, for each and every one of you who is reading these words. Blessings, friends.

GET BACK INTO YOUR HEART

Chapter 41

Good morning, friends. There is always a moment of reception, a moment in which the channel comes home to his heart. And this is the place to be, friends. You might say, "I want to go here, I want to go there. I want to do this, I want to do that." But we tell you that the place you need to go to is your heart. You need to settle in there. And then you can enjoy the journey, yes?

We are going to be quite direct and tell the channel, while telling you as well, that for most of you, it is not enough to settle into your heart in the morning and then to go about your day.

You must resettle into your heart over and over and
over again, multiple times during the day.

This needs to be your practice. For if you do not do that, then it is likely that you will not be there enough of the time. And so this is what we are telling the channel. And this is what we are telling you as well. It is not enough to get up, to get into your heart, and then to go about your day. That is a great beginning! Along with that, throughout your day, you must also do the mini retreats that we have spoken about many times.

This is the practice for today, friends. And by doing so, it will become very natural to you to spend most of your waking hours in your heart centers, yes? And every practice that we share with you comes out of this. It comes out of being settled into your heart. Without that, there can be no other practice. And this is why we will give you this practice over and over again until we are sure that you and the channel get it.

The morning, friends, is the time to reacquaint yourself with your heart, yes? To get back in there, yes? So that you might say as the channel is now saying to himself, "Ah! This is it. Okay, I am home now. Now I have my baseline for the day. When I notice that I am not in my heart, I might return to it over and over again until I am there all the time, no matter where I am, no matter what I am doing." Those are the words that we want you to remember today, friends: "No matter where I am and no matter what I am doing."

Let there be no conditions that you put upon yourself for being in your heart, for being open in a state of love.

Do you see what we mean by that, friends? Your mind might place lots of conditions on being settled into your heart and being settled into the love that is within yourself. Let go of all of these! Let your love be *un*-conditional. For the very first time, the channel is really getting that word now: *un*-conditional!

Place no conditions upon your intention, commitment, and devotion to tuning into the great love within you. Experience the joy of being in that space, independent of conditions. This is what the channel is currently focusing on right now along his path. We will put it one more way before we go. It cannot be, "I will be settled into my heart and tuned into the great love that is within me *if…*" No, no, no. It cannot be like that. It cannot be, "*If* I am in this particular place, *if* I am doing this particular thing, *if* I am with this particular person, *if* nobody is bothering me at the current time …" No, no no. It cannot be like that. It must be forever and always. And then you will experience the kingdom of heaven that is within you. We say that with no religious context. For there is no religion here as part of these teachings.

> *There is only universal truth. That is it.*
> *There is nothing more than that.*

And there is nothing at all that is less than that. It is whole and complete as a universal teaching that comes from the heart of all hearts.

We do not know if we have even used this word "challenge" before, friends, but we will use it today. Challenge yourself to re-tune to the greatness of your heart throughout your day without condition. Make it a little bit of a fun test: how much time during the day can I truly be present in my heart space without condition? And how devoted can I be to returning there over and over, as often as is necessary during my day? Let it not be a serious practice, my friends. None of these practices are serious at all. Let it be a fun one with no judgment placed upon yourself. Do not say, "Oh no! I am not in my heart right now. To hell with me!" Do not do that, friends. Let it be fun. Let it be with joy. For everything you do in your life, from our perspective, should be done out of fun and out of joy.

And if you say to yourself, "that is impossible," we say that once you have read the book, it will become possible. You will be able to guide yourself in that direction. And then you will be able to say to yourself, "Ah yes, life is meant to be fun and joyful. And that is how I am experiencing it now because I am embodying the teachings of The Teachers of The Light."

All of the teachings blossom from the essential teaching of being present in your heart center.

It is enough, is it not? To get your juices flowing? To get you excited? You might say to yourself, "Well this is not very exciting." We say it is, friends. We say it is incredibly exciting to be in your heart space. We would even say that it is a way of turning yourself on. We would say it is a way of being turned on into a state of pleasure. Do you see, friends, the pleasure that is found is found by being in your heart? And there is nothing more exciting than that.

Stay loose, my friends. We are telling that to the channel. Move your bodies. Sing, dance, run, play, skip, hop! Do whatever it is you need to do to get out of your heads, to keep your minds flexible and open, and to keep your bodies flexible and loose. Let go of your rigidity. It will not be needed where you are going. And that is not meant to be a riddle, friends. It means where you are going, *dimensionally* speaking. We are not speaking about leaving your bodies. We are saying that the rigidity is not needed to experience the great love, the great light, the great joy, and the great freedom that is within you, and is ready to be experienced in this incarnation in which you find yourselves.

That is it for today, friends! It is with great joy in our hearts and a big smile on our light body faces, that we say, as we always do, that we have great, great, great love for you. And we wish for you to feel that love. And there are many teachings in the book that are directed towards that, towards opening you up to experiencing the love that we have for you, that the universe has for you, that creator him-herself has for you. We will leave it at that, friends. Blessings!

WHAT GOD WANTS

Chapter 42

Dear ones, we are going to say something quite bold. You do not serve your purpose on this planet, nor do you serve the purpose of creation, by shining dimly. You were meant to shine bright!

Friends, have you ever looked up to the night sky, and one particular star was shining brighter than all the others? This is the level of brightness with which you were meant to shine, every one of you. Every practice that we have given you in this book is meant to support you so that you may shine as bright as this particular star that we speak of.

Dear friends, there are many on this planet who would like to tell you what god wants from you, yes? Simply by saying that, many come into your mind. So we do not need to get into details with you. For each of you, perhaps, has had different people in your lives who have told you what god wants from you. And perhaps some of you have had none at all so you have no clue. You have had to go at it on your own. You have had to try to figure it out for yourself. So we will tell you, from our perspective, what god wants of you.

*Very simply, god wants you to shine like the star that you are
and wants you to reflect the godliness that is within
him-her, right back to him-her.*

He-she wants you to be a pure reflection of what he-she is.

Friends, we use this word "he-she," but the creator that we speak of is not limited in any way, shape, or form by the gender identity you might conceive. We use this terminology to be politically correct and to infer that god is neither male nor female. And if anything, god is both, yes? To some, this might seem like blasphemy to say. But all we can do is share our truth. And as we have said before, if it resonates with you, that is wonderful. And if not, then we encourage you to simply let it go. And then perhaps it will become your truth as well, some day.

So now do you see, friends, what god wants of you? That is it. By now, we do hope you know that god is every good quality that you can ever think of. And every quality that is within god is within you as well. And to make god happy, to make god smile, all you have to do is reflect that back to him-her. Let him-her see who you are! Let him-her see that you know there is great godliness within you.

It pleases creator when you express this godliness out in the world, friends, that is what makes creator smile. From our perspective, friends, creator does not want you to live boxed in by rules or laws.

*Creator wants you to experience the freedom of
being the creator-god that you are.*

And so it is we say that any rules or laws handed down through creator to a particular teacher, were simply meant to point you in the right direction.

Certainly you might say to yourself, friends, that god is love and thus there are certain things that god would not do. So from our perspective, any laws or any rules that have been passed down were meant to reflect this truth, were meant to guide you to the love that is within you, so that you might act out of this love, for yourself and for all others around you, yes? So we say if you are going to give yourself a commandment, let it be that. Let it be to always act out of the principle force of love that is within you. Let it be to always think and to act out of love, out of the great love within you, the same great love that is within creator him-herself. If you do that, it is very difficult to do wrong. And if you do wrong, or what you label as "wrong," that is fine too. All you need to do is start from today and to choose to think and act out of love today. Then you will please creator.

Creator is incredibly forgiving, friends.

Creator is not vengeful. This is a myth. And so it is, if you were misguided yesterday, and did not think or act out of love, you can change that today. And thus, you will have left yesterday behind. You will be shining bright like the star you were meant to be, again. Thus you will serve your purpose on the planet. You will serve creation, and creator will be pleased. Creator will smile upon you.

Do you see, friends, that our energy is such that we will always do our very best to never pass judgment on anybody at all? We create space for all to reside. We do our very best to speak out of love. This is what we are asking you to do as well.

Do your very best to think, to speak, and to act out of love. And in this way, you are fulfilling your purpose. You are fulfilling the purpose of creation. It is that simple.

We feel like we have already given you quite a bit of insight on how to react, and how not to react, to those who are not acting out of love. Be loving whenever possible. And most of the time, it is possible to be loving, and to respond in a loving way. This is how the evolution of humanity progresses in a positive manner, by shifting as many thoughts, as many words, and as many actions as you can, back to love.

You do not need to repay creator for creation. It is creator's gift to you. And it is a selfless gift. Creator created for the sake of love. We would say it was in creator's heart to create, so creator created! And here you are! How wonderful! Nothing would please creator more than for you to shine like the star you are, to reflect your godliness to all. For creator is in all, yes? And so really, this is the teaching for today, friends. The creator that we speak of is not isolated to something that is outside of you or outside of creation.

Creator is everywhere and in everything.

Creator thought it would be quite mischievous to place him-herself there, within everything. Creator thought it would be quite playful to do it this way. And so here we all are, friends. And if you sit for long enough, friends, you will know where creator is. So now we wish you many blessings, friends. We encourage you to stay as light, and as joyful, and as loving as possible today and every day. Blessings.

SUPREME CREATOR

Chapter 43

Friends, there are many different ways in which you can view creation, and all ways are welcome here. There is no right and there is no wrong. But we will simply offer you our perspective. And if it resonates with you, it might become your perspective as well. Or you might utilize our perspective to add to your perspective, or perhaps to take away from your perspective. Do you see? We do not wish to force our perspective upon you. If it resonates with you, great. If not, that is fine as well. We simply share because some of you would like us to share, from our perspective, how we see creation. And the channel too, has been asking us recently. And so we will share it with you in this way.

There is an origin point that you might call the supreme creator. And from this origin point, supreme creator expanded him-herself in all directions and put him-herself everywhere and in everything. And so it is that now creator is found throughout the universe. There is nowhere that creator is not. And this includes within you, and it includes within all of your brothers and sisters, and it includes within every life form that you see on this planet. So now you see that all is god, right? There is godliness within all. That is the way it is from our perspective. And that is the channel's perspective as well.

Everything is sacred. Everything is beautiful. Everything is divine. How can it not be? Creator is everywhere and everything. It is just the way it is.

And so you might look back. And we say "look back" because we know that is the best way your logic will understand it, and simply say, "Thank you. I will do my best to honor your creation by serving my purpose within it, by being as loving as I can to all beings everywhere knowing that you, supreme creator, is within all." And that, my friends, will please supreme creator greatly. That will put a smile on creator's face. And what will make creation complete, is when all life forms that are part of creation know themselves as who they are, when all know the godliness that is within them, and that is flowing within all. Then the kingdom of heaven (remember, with no religious context) is present for all to experience. This is creator's vision. You are here to fulfill it. And what a gift it is, friends, yes?

Do you see now that creation is a gift?

It is a gift from supreme creator and has been given to you. It is a great blessing. It is a great blessing to be part of it, to be actively participating in it, to be actively participating in the great awakening that is happening now, the return to love that is happening now, the return to fulfilling the supreme creator's promise to all now. The promise is that all shall know themselves for who they are. And now you know who you are. If you have yet to experience it, you have at least received a taste of it through your sacred retreat. And the vibration that is inherent in the words that we speak through the channel today points you in the right direction, so that you begin to get it.

We are very happy to have brought you this transmission today, friends. The channel has been asking for it and so we have given it to him. And we give it to you as well. Dear ones, we tell you it is a great blessing to receive this transmission. It is by the grace of creator him-herself that it is received and transmitted through the channel and that it is now received by you. It comes straight from creator. It comes straight from the heart of creator to your heart. This is what creator says.

The channel has a soul contract, as you do all. And in that soul contract, it is written that the supreme creator will speak through him to others. It is happening now through us, The Teachers of The Light. We are the intermediaries. But this particular transmission comes from an even higher place, closer to the supreme creator. And with it, you receive the blessings of supreme creator. And we do as well. And the channel does as well. We all do. We are all blessed.

So accept the blessing, friends, with gratitude, with humility, and respect. For we tell you that the transmissions that are coming through the channel have been prepared for a long time. He himself, on a soul level, has had many incarnations, all leading up to this one. Through it, he is able to share the message of supreme creator through us, The Teachers of The Light, and with you. We do this all in the name of love, and all in the name of service. And we tell you friends, that if supreme creator had a message for you, which he-she does, it is very simple: It is to live your light. It is to live the living light that is within you. In this way, you are serving the purpose of creation.

HEAVEN ON EARTH

Chapter 44

Dear ones, we would like you to take a moment to feel the magnitude of what we have just shared with you in our prior transmission. Do you see now, friends, that god is not outside of yourself? Do you see now that god is within yourself?

And so it is, that this is the direction we have been pointing you in from day one. And so whatever we have shared with you in our prior transmission, is meant to serve you in this way. It is meant to serve as another means to share the truth that we know with you: what you seek is within yourself, and thus you must go inside to find it. And there it is, waiting for you.

And in that moment, when you discover that creator is within you, you know too that creator is within all.

And it becomes an experience, not just a knowing. In fact, we would say that you can only know by experience, yes?

And so we tell you, friends, that we have given you everything you need. And now it is simply about the practice. And although we have shared many practices with you, it is all part of the same one practice, just as we are all part of the same one source, and just as that one source is within us all.

The practice is to go within and to find what it is you are seeking inside yourself. And then, everything you are seeking outside of yourself will come to fruition as well. This is the way it goes. And this is why, for the last time we will say, that the kingdom of heaven is within you, not without! But once you discover it within yourself, it will appear right in front of you, in front of your very own eyes. It will become manifest in front of you because you have discovered it within you.

And so it is, friends, that our work with you is now complete. But friends, do you see that the work that we are doing with you never ends? It continues by way of your practice. And so it is friends, there are some of you who will close the book and that will be that. You will say to yourselves, "Well, I have tried the practices a little bit here and there. I do not see much of a result from them so that is that. I will go on with my life. It will be as it will be." There are others of you who have had enough of a taste of it, enough of a taste of the great love, the great light of the creator that is within you, that you will be inspired enough to continue the practices, yes? And it is through this devotion, through this commitment, that you will reap all of the blessings creator has in store for you.

If there was one more thing that the supreme creator would like to say to you, he-she would say that his-her desire is for you to experience the godliness that is within you, and to reflect that back to every person on this planet, and to experience the great heavenly paradise that is available for you to experience in the physical form that you are in now. We know that these are very strong words, friends. For some they might seem a bit much. But we speak the truth as we see it, as we hear it, and as we experience it. And that is all we can do.

What we want you to know the most, friends, is that we have great love for you. We see the great potential that every human being has on this planet to know the great love and the great light that is within them, to know the creator, the god-self that is within them, that is within all. We see this potential in each and every one of you, not just a chosen few.

And so it is that we ask you to allow the belief that we have in you to encourage you to believe in yourself, and to believe that anything is possible on this planet.

It is that belief, which we see as truth, that will create shifts on this planet that you have never seen before, and that perhaps you did not even think were possible until now.

Our prediction, friends, is that all will live in peace, and that all will live in love, and that all will live in respect, and that all will live in harmony, and that all will know the godliness that is within them and within all, without any prejudice and without any separation, quite soon. This is the direction you are going. This is the river upon which you are flowing. There is no stopping it now. It has too much momentum to stop. So celebrate this friends, yes?

Celebrate the direction that you are all moving in.

And remember the words that we have spoken many times: "It is happening, it is happening, it is happening." Be bold enough to see beyond what it is you see with your eyes. Things are changing. Things are shifting. All are returning to love.

We are now complete with our teachings. And it is with great love, with great gratitude, and great appreciation, that we say thank you for being open to the vibration which we have shared with you. For that is all that we have ever asked of you, is to be open. And what we see is that many of you have done that. We are looking backwards from a future timeline to all of those who have read this book. And we see that most of you have stayed open. You have stayed curious. And now you must carry on in that direction. You must carry on and fulfill the potential that we see for all of you.

And so it is that we thank the channel as well. For he did not have to sit, on multiple mornings, and allow himself to receive these transmissions to share with you. But he was told, quite early on, that this is of great importance. And so he allowed us to speak through him, he allowed the energy to flow through him, to be a receiver and a transmitter.

Dear ones, we are going to leave you with this. There is a miracle at hand. It is god's creation. It is the supreme creator's creation. And you are part of it. And not only are you part of it, but you *are* it!

You are the creation and you are creator him-herself.

That is the miracle, friends. Celebrate it. It is truly miraculous. It is truly spectacular!

We are going to say what we are about to say, not to do advertising on behalf of the channel, but rather to push him onwards with his spiritual journey, to push him to continue to be of service in this way. For it is still unknown to us how things will proceed from this day onwards. We do not know if he will gather around with three or four people, or three or four hundred people to share the vibration that we have shared with him. So we simply encourage you to look and see what offerings he is giving so that you may continue to have an experience with us.

And do not be shy about re-reading every transmission in this book if you feel like that would be of benefit to you! Do not be shy about picking it up every once in a while, and opening up to a page, and to trust that that page is meant for you on that particular day of your life. Do not be shy about sharing this material with others who you think might be open to it, and who you think might not be open to it. Because in actuality they might be open to it!

It is all about spreading the love, friends, yes? It is all about waking as many people up as possible to the great love and the great light that is within them. And soon all will have been awakened. And you will be living on a planet of light. And everybody's light will be shining so brightly, that the entire galaxy will be shining from the light that is coming out of your hearts.

We see it now, friends. This is happening already. But we see it multiplying and multiplying until everyone's heart has been turned on. As usual, we have extended our stay as we have done multiple times. We have said that we would be leaving you with something and then we keep going! So now we will say for the final time, friends: Keep going. Continue to awaken. That is it.

Other Books by Darren

Create Your Dream Life Now:
A Workbook & Guide for Manifesting Your Destiny

Journey of the Heart: Awakening To Love:
Channeling The Teachers of The Light

Website

www.awakenwithdarren.com

Contact

DarrenMarc111@gmail.com

www.ingramcontent.com/pod-product-compliance
Lightning Source LLC
Chambersburg PA
CBHW051149130726
47988CB00005B/2055